Chronicles of Jane

Vol 2

KAMELAH BLAIR

Copyright © 2021 Kamelah Blair

All rights reserved. Printed in the United States of America. No part of this book may be used or reproduced in any manner whatsoever without written permission except in the case of brief quotations embodied in critical articles or reviews.

ISBN: 9798539246648

Published by: Daughter of the King Publishing

The Missing Pieces

Chapters 1-11

End of Vol 1

The last line (of book one) says "there's a fourth piece of luggage in the master bedroom closet, you can use it. What happens next as a whole story"

Beginning of Vol 2

KAMELAH BLAIR

The phoenix rising from the ashes depicts who Kamelah Blair is. She was born and raised in Toronto, Ontario, and lived within the community of Jane and Finch. Jane Street was a tight-knit, urban community with a mix of middle and upper-class families filled with intelligence and street smarts.

Kamelah is the CEO of four successful companies and a mother of two. She graduated from George Brown College with an Honors Diploma in Medical Administration and Blood Lab Technician.

The stone that the builders refused was what she used to build her empire. She is known as the black sheep on her mother's side of the family and the only college graduate on her father's side of the family. Her uncle, grandmother, godmother, father, and stepmother encouraged her to be better than the negative things said to her.

Since VO1, she has become certified in Life Coaching and Digital Marketing from Google. She has also expanded the COJ brand by adding appeal.

Table of Contents

Chapter 1: The Decision — 1

Chapter 2: Broken Bondage — 13

Chapter 3: Paid for Freedom — 17

Chapter 4: Art of Life — 25

Chapter 5: Family, Respect & Travels — 37

Chapter 6: Kind Troubles — 49

Chapter 7: Say a Prayer or Two — 65

Chapter 8: Sticks and Stones — 73

Chapter 9: A Couple of Couples — 83

Chapter 10: Broken Glass — 95

Chapter 11: Blackouts — 103

CHAPTER 1:

THE DECISION

I just stood there for a while staring at the money in the apartment that Frank led me to. I took off my hat, and sweater. I moved some of the cash off the sofa and sat there for a while. Frank called a few times. I never answered, I just texted back and said, "I'll call you back shortly, everything is ok." Around 3 am, I made up my mind to basically pack up all of the cash. I went for the luggage set and while packing the cash, I noticed that not all of the cash was in Canadian currency. It was an assortment of US Dollars, British pounds and Canadian dollars.

Being the organized person that I am, I said to myself, "I'm going to put all the American on the loveseat. I'm going to put all the Canadian on the sofa, and all the pounds in a pile on the left." Midway through doing that, Frank called me again and I answered. He asked if I was okay and I told him everything was fine.

He then went on to tell me that he didn't want the Canadian currency, he just wanted the British Pounds and the US dollars. Well naturally I asked him, "What would you want to do with the Canadian currency?"

He said, "That will be for a later conversation." I hung up and put the money together. This took me until 7 am. The Canadian currency I just left on the floor close to the sofa. The Canadian currency was more than the American without it being converted. I went to the kitchen and made myself a cup of tea. Now that there was space, I got a blanket from the linen closet. I just sat there for a while and fell asleep.

When I woke up, it was around 1:30 pm in the afternoon. I had to wait for it to get dark, so I just continued to sit and I watched TV. I had a few missed calls from my babysitter who was watching the kids and from my neighbor because I had her car. I just texted them and let them know, "I'm fine and I'll be there shortly. I called a friend that worked in the mall and asked them to drop off some dinner. I instructed her to let me talk to the kids when they came home. Frank called me a few times. In one of our phone calls, we discussed where I would drop the money. Of course Frank, being as difficult as he was, didn't want all the money to be left in the same location.

In this phone call he said, "Whatever the Canadian currency comes to, take half."

I asked him, "You don't know what the amount is?"

He replied, "I stopped counting after $100,000." We tried our best to keep our phone conversation short.

I just relaxed while I was there. Frank and I had a good relationship. At any given time, I was never scared. To be honest, I just wanted to go home, even though the apartment was very comfortable and quiet. I just wanted to be in my own space. Even while sitting there, I was thinking, what am I going to do with this other half that now belongs to me?

I then received a text from Frank telling me where to drop off the US currency - in Montreal.

In the text, he told me that I have a choice to drive a vehicle I arrange to get my hands on or he could rent a car for me to drive. But, he made it clear that I was NOT to take a plane. So, I texted him back and I asked how quickly he wanted this money. He said, "Like yesterday." Keep in mind that I had my two children that I had to deal with and they were left with a babysitter. So, I had to explain to him that if he wanted it and he wanted it quickly, why didn't he say that earlier considering I hadn't even made arrangements and I'd already been there almost 24 hours?! After telling him 2 or 5 Jamaican bad words, we agreed that this was not going to work. I took one of the suitcases with me, turned off the tv and lights, locked the door, and went home.

Two days later, I got someone to rent a car. I got a group of friends together and just said, "You know what? Let's just have a girl's trip." I tried to find an excuse on why I needed to go to Montreal. Keep in mind, I don't speak French all that well. Although I could understand some of it, this would be the first time I'd ever gone to Montreal.

Everybody was rustling, "Oh we don't have enough funds to go..." or "We'll have to get babysitters..."

I just volunteered, "We'll have one babysitter." We had an elderly lady that lived nearby. She didn't mind, and her rate was for the day. At the time, it was $40 a day per child. All together collectively, it would have been five children. So, I paid her, even though my boys would be with their grandmother from their father's side most of the time. So, we were off on our road trip to Montreal!

We got to Montreal and went to the hotel. I let the girls stay in the car when I got to the hotel. I didn't rent the hotel in my real name. It was a double suite so the doors opened in the middle - that way we would have enough space. This time, Frank had called me so many times and I only texted him back once to tell him that I was on my way. And, that I'd call him when I got there. Everyone got something to eat and all the ladies got comfortable. I stepped away from them and went to the lobby. Mind you, this was in the Presidential Suite.

The front desk asked me, "Miss, are you okay?"

I said, "Yes, I'm just taking in the scenery and my friends are all asleep. I just need some privacy for a phone call." She let me know that I could go into a board meeting room if I needed to take a call. I said, "Yes actually, that would be nice. It's a business call." They told me there's a computer and fax machine in there - back then it would have been either an IBM computer or a Dell computer. I told them I needed a pen and paper. I went in there and had a conversation with Frank.

Frank then gave me the address and I wrote it down. Something I learned on a TV show was that when you write on a notepad, depending on how hard you press, what you write goes under at least three to four pages. When I tore off the address, I actually turned back and I took the notepad with me. I then took half of the sheets from the notepad and left the bottom half. So, if anything had pressed through, I would have that evidence with me.

In the morning while we were at breakfast, I asked a waitress where the address was and about how far it was from the hotel, of course, giving her a different street number. She said, "Oh, it's approximately 15 minutes from here." She gave me directions -you know, turn left here... then turn right there... In addition to this, she listed the street names. I didn't want to ask the front staff or any staff there about the address just to cover my tracks. I then spoke to Frank again and I let him know that we'd be going there in the afternoon when we planned to do some sightseeing or do some shopping.

Then he asked me, "What do you mean by "We'?"

I said, "Well I made this a girl's trip."

He said, "You know what? Well, buy the girls something."

I said, "I can't buy everybody something too lavish."

He explained, "Just buy them a keepsake." You know, that was my intention anyway.

So I brought everybody back to the hotel and I told them that I would be back. I was going to meet somebody, but they never questioned me. I guess being tired from our ups and downs for the day, I did not have to worry about their questions. The treatment they were receiving from the hotel was such that if they wanted anything, they could get it. The hotel had amenities that they could enjoy without me being present for 15 minutes, as the waitress said.

I let Frank know that I was on my way. We stayed on the phone and we were silent the whole 15 minutes ride. I could hear him shuffling and I could hear music playing in his background, but I was just paying attention to the road. When I got there, the car stopped and he asked, "Did you reach?"

I said, "Yeah."

He replied, "It's nice, isn't it?"

I said, "Yes". It was a castle-like home in an upscale neighborhood. It had this old rustic look to it, but it was nice.

Then Frank said, "Hold on a second, let me call somebody to come out." That day, I was wearing a green, black and yellow track suit. I had on a hat, but I removed it while driving then promptly put it back on and adjusted it so that my eyes couldn't be seen too much. I saw this petite Indian lady coming towards me and Frank said, "Do you see the lady? Her name is Harp." While she was walking up this long driveway, he kept talking, "Harp, helped me out a lot in the past. So really, if you ever need anything while you're there, you could always call on her. I would rather you guys stay there, but I know how you are. You probably would have declined the invitation to stay there anyways."

Harp came up and she greeted me and she wanted to hug but I was resistant. Somehow we ended up hugging, and she asked me if I was okay. She asked how long I'd been in Montreal. I told her for two days. Then she told me some places that I had to go check out. The places that Harp suggested to me included art galleries, art shows, museums and other stuff that was never in my plan for this girl's trip, Plus, I'm hood, what I was doing there I didn't know. But, it was the thought that counted with Harp - that's just how she was.

Then she began describing some stores I actually had passed, but they were high-end stores. She said she just purchased this necklace at this jewelry store and if I ever needed jewelry while I was in Montreal, I could get it from this man who was from Italy. I told her I wasn't too fond of jewelry, but mentioned it was a very nice piece around her neck. I opened the trunk and I asked her if she'd be okay to bring it in and she said, "Can you bring it for me?" Of course I was hesitant at first- I wasn't scared- it was just that the atmosphere was so nice and the way I was dressed made me feel out of place.

However, I took out the suitcase and I locked the car doors with the remote. I continued to walk up the driveway. While I was walking up, I could see an elderly Indian man waving like he was happy to see me. About midway in the driveway Harp said to me, "Frank speaks so highly of you. He's a really good friend of mine too. Very nice gentleman."

I kind of sided with her and said, "Yes, I know, he's very nice." All the while keeping in mind that Frank was still on the phone in my pocket, listening in silence. I think that I forgot to hang it up.

He had a thing where he chuckles. I began to faintly hear that chuckle of his and said, "Oh Frank's still on the phone!"

Harp took the phone from me and said to Frank, "She's a nice young lady. Is she your girlfriend?"

I shut that down immediately, "Absolutely, not! Nothing like that! We're just good friends."

She continued talking with him, "Well, you know what? You should marry her..." I had to shut Harp down.

When we got to the door, the old man also greeted me with a hug. They were like , "Do you want to stay for dinner? Come in, come in." I was standing in the doorway, taking it all in. They had grand staircases on both sides with a big table in the middle and I could see the helpers in the house. They passed by one or two times while they were preparing for dinner. I felt bad to decline their offer to stay for dinner, but I told her that I had friends that I had come with.

She said, "Well you and your friends could come for dinner."

I told her, "I'd have to ask them because we had prior arrangements."

Then she asked me, "Do you want the suitcase back?"

I replied, "I'm not too sure what Frank wants with a suitcase."

She said, "I travel a lot, I have a lot of suitcases, I'm going to have a mismatched piece. I don't want to have that. Just come in and I'll be back." Then her help brought me to the left of the house. I wasn't sure if it was the living room, or just a sitting area where there were multiple pieces of art. I'm not the best art person, I just knew they looked rich and their furniture was luxurious red velvet with gold piping. You could tell that the area rug was hand-woven. I was taking in all these details in this particular room, just imagining how much dusting the helpers had to do weekly and what the rest of this house could possibly look like.

I was inside for all of 10 minutes. She brought back a suitcase and brought back a couple of business cards. She said to me, "These are some places I want you to visit while you're in Montreal." She gave me a list of mostly the art galleries and museums she had been speaking of. She said, "If you end up going to these places, tell them I sent you. They can give you the best treatment."

She asked me again if I was okay, and I replied, "Yes, I am fine." She proceeded to ask if my friends were okay, and I replied, "I am sure that they are fine."

She then passed me a gift bag. It had a gift box in it from what I could see through the tissue paper. She said, "Don't open my gift to you until you get home."

I asked her to clarify, "Do you mean my home as in the hotel in Montreal? Or my home back in Toronto?"

She said, "Either one. Just don't open it until you get inside. It was nice to meet you. If you do change your mind and come, you don't even have to call." I didn't know her number anyway, but she and I were on the same wavelength of not sharing contact information. She continued, "You can just come. I don't have many visitors. I'll know that it's you."

She wished me well and then sent me off. While she was closing the door and I was going down the steps to leave, she said, "Your children will be well, don't worry. You worry a lot."

I said, "Pardon?"

She repeated, 'Know that your children will be well."

I was puzzled, "Frank told you about my kids?" I said this with a smile.

She said, "I told you, Frank speaks highly of you." I told her thank you and wished her well. As I got back in the car, I just focused on remembering my way back to the hotel. On the way to the hotel, I saw one of the museums. Mind you, my friends don't know how to act, so while passing the museum, I parked the car and I went just to look. The museum was almost closed, but I went in and I was looking around. I'd never been to an art museum before, so I was just looking at the pictures.

While I was looking at the pictures, a man asked, "Good afternoon. What do you see?" We were looking at a cluster of 8x10 pictures among a lot of art on the wall.

This particular 8x10 picture captured me at that moment. The photo was just a silhouette of a lady. Her back was naked, but she had on a skirt. She was looking off into the distance, but off to the right in the distance were just colors. When this gentleman asked me what I saw, the first thing that I noticed was her wristwatch that she had on. He said, "Funny enough, there's only been a few people that came in here who noticed that she's wearing a watch. Most people are attracted to the colors."

He introduced himself, "Hi, my name is Richard." I said to him, "Hi, my name is Kristine. Harp sent me here." His demeanor changed and he called his staff. They gave me water that was in a glass bottle. All of a sudden, everybody got busy. Richard took me down a hallway and showed me these other art pieces. He also went to another room where the people were working with clay to make art pieces. He showed me where they put the figures to dry. He basically gave me a detailed tour just because I told him that Harp sent me. Richard also asked me, "Did you go to the jewelry store?" He was sending me to the same places as if it was a routine and it was all part of a tour one should take.

I told him, "No, this was my first stop."

He said, "Well you cannot leave here without seeing these places." He began to show me the prices of the art pieces in the gallery. We're talking $10,000, $20,000 & $30,000 pieces, that really looked so simple. I was in that gallery for probably 20 minutes. Upon leaving, he assured me that I should still go and get the experience at the other places. But to be honest, halfway through all that he said, all that was on my mind was "What did Harp give me?"

CHAPTER 2:

BROKEN BONDAGE

I was 18 when I first got pregnant. And, at eighteen I was introduced into a life of fraud. I had always lived on my own and I became the person where if you needed something, you would have to come to me first. Even though there were bigger heads, I was introduced to the kingpin of the game, or so he thought.

At first, I would just observe the content and the mistakes. Eventually, I had to do the work while making it look relevant to the 90's, because what they were doing was very 70's and 80's. At this time, technology was coming out and you could imagine what it was like back in 1996 when the internet was just coming out. Because I went to school, I was more knowledgeable about these things so they would pay someone a lot of cash to do the work. Soon, they were relying on me to get it done and paying me much more as I could get it done in a timely manner along with answering consistent questions about the computers, fonts, paper, thickness, etc.

In that same week, there was a big concert coming up and my dad received two free VIP passes. They were bringing up about 3 big artists that made up the Jamaican culture. Everybody wanted to go in our circle and they were mad asking us, "How come you got only one ticket? You didn't get five or six?" This bickering went on for some time. While holding my VIP pass, my mind went to a place I never came back from. It was the first big thing that I did when it came to fraud.

I asked one of the people that were in the house to give me a ride. We took that VIP pass and went to Staples. I got the red ones because of the VIP concert. I color photocopied it, and laminated the copies. We sold a bunch to his friends and they ended up selling them out back in the streets for their own profit. There were three or four friends that just came up from Jamaica, so we actually gifted them the VIP passes and told them to sell them and keep the money. We made a lot of money that day.

I didn't go to the concert, I was tired from the day. By the time everybody got to the concert, the promoters were seeing what was going on. The VIP section was already full, and tickets were over capacity. There was nobody in the general section, everybody was in the VIP. So they figured out hours into the concert that something was wrong. So they started to stop people with VIP passes. But, there was nothing they could do at the time because to the naked eye, there was no fault. They didn't have a count of how much was given. People were coming from America, England and from Jamaica - they didn't know where the passes were coming from. With that money, I refurbished my new apartment with some different styles that came from Italy. I went on vacation and I put some of it away with the other money that I won with the baby contest.

I became the person with the links. One process became another process. Now the streets knew that if something was needed that I could be linked

. That got my name out there to the bigger people. They asked how we even thought of that and could we do this again? "Absolutely not," was my answer.

The heat was on us because people were saying, "I got my ticket from so and so". It was a bus in the streets. Although the promoters never came directly to us, it was a learning lesson for them and a bus in the street to this day.

I took a few jobs from the bigger heads from time to time when they asked but, I made it clear, I only wanted to be behind the scenes. I was still attending school and from time to time, I would have flashbacks of Jermaine and the shooting that would send me into days of silence and not wanting to talk to anyone. I would just listen to music or take a flight so I could be alone above ground to try and release my feelings.

I was receiving the cash and I could travel when I wanted to, but I had to be smart. I was still a student that was also on the system. I had a part-time job that paid me cash at the same hairdresser I used to go to. It started as a co-op program and then became one of my cover ups.

I was raised to always be well dressed so it never came off as being a flash and it never caught anyone's eye that I had more than what they really knew. While I was in high school, I still took a course for microcomputers at a private college just to take OSAP. I didn't need it, but I did need another coverup. I completed the course and I also got more advanced from what I already knew. I gifted myself with a green and silver Lexus. Mind you, I was 17 years old. When everyone asked about it, I told them I used the money from my student loan and I financed it. This was not strange as everyone used their loans to buy things to level them up.

I never had a license. That time it was a 360 that you could get while you were in high school and with that 360 you were able to drive. But that was just yet another way to be traced, so I never got it. I paid my rent for two years in advance. When the landlord asked why, I explained to him that my grandmother had passed and left me with some money and in 2 years, I would be done with school and did not want to worry about bills. I would give a few of my friends and family $200 or $500 to get on their feet or just to get themselves together.

This did not set off any red flags as people knew my godmother had money and my parents were in the streets and cash was always easy to get. One of the bigger heads went to jail overseas so it slowed down things for a few people. I then took on the role as the middle man, as I wanted no part of the controversy that was around the bigger head and his court case. I began to let people know that I knew a person that could get things done for them. My people were not around anymore and I had no links at the moment. This allowed me to have the power to increase the prices. It would make up for the loss of not having as much work. I had accumulated so much cash. This in spite of the fact that I was still spending money to pay for things daily for my friends and I, as a normal teen would.

CHAPTER 3:

PAID FOR FREEDOM

Goldy and I had gotten into a heated argument that stayed on my mind for a few weeks and so I came up with a plan to ease my mind. Of course, I took a vacation with me and my thoughts. She still lived in the apartment that she had called the police on me in, causing me to have to go to Covenant House. Nearly a month after clearing my mind, I went to school early. I had on a Nike blue, white and black tracksuit with the latest Penny Hardaway sneakers to match. I went to the computer lab and started searching on the internet. I researched the year that I was born and what it cost at the time to have a child if you were from Canada. It didn't give me an accurate amount, so I asked around. I even asked the health teachers. They didn't give me an accurate number but did give me a ballpark number of what it would cost as a refugee in the same year I was born. It was close to what the internet was saying even though I never mentioned to anyone that I was a refugee. Still, I went with it and went on to ask yet another question to my health teacher. "Miss, what would a refugee have to pay if it was last year?" She asked me why I was asking. I lied and said that it was for a social studies class about refugees and child services.

The number that kept on coming up was between $20-$30,000. So that afternoon, I left an hour early and I went home and counted out $35,000 cash. I called my dad and my godmother and I told them to meet me at my mom's building because I needed to have a conversation with her. My mother lived three buildings down from me, in the core of Jane and Finch, and didn't even know it. Of course, my godmother was happy because she thought it was about the reconciliation that we needed. My dad said he would be a little bit late. My godmother was way too early as I knew she would be. At that time, she drove a burgundy Cadillac with a tan interior and she had no clue where I lived. If she ever knew that I lived in Jane and Finch, she never would have approved and it would have been a long ride back to Newmarket. But, my dad was dating a lady who lived in Mississauga and my godmother was sure that's where we lived.

I was waiting for my dad and getting upset that he was late. I needed him to be there so that he could drive with me after, but I also did not want to be there this long, so I went on without him. Exiting the elevator and looking down the hallway gave me an instant flashback and I became angry, but I did not want my godmother to see me get out of hand, so I clenched my teeth as she knocked on the door.

She invited us in and of course, I didn't go far. I remained at her door. My mother said to me, "You can have a seat."

I said, "No, it's okay. I can stand up."

Then my godmother started to talk and pray and say, "I prayed for this day, for a long period of time." She said another prayer. I did not fully close my eyes though, as the last scene of me being here replayed over and over each time I blinked. I felt my heart begin to race. The door wasn't far from her dining table. My godmother sat a little bit further from me and began the conversation with, "We have been waiting for this day for years…" I cut her off after a while because I knew where she was going with it, and I didn't want to disappoint her.

I said to her that "I never really came here for this. I know what you want but it's not what I want to do."

"What are you talking about?" my mother asked. I explained, "I don't want nobody to have a thing over me in life. And I feel the only thing this lady has over me is that she gave me life." I said it with pride and bass in my voice, but I was not looking at either of them.

"That conversation that you guys want me to have, I refuse to have it. I never asked to be here. You got married to my father. Whatever problem you guys had should not be mine." I could see my mom starting to sweat. She was getting furious, but she couldn't get as angry because of course, my godmother was there. Which was all in my initial plan. She couldn't even curse a bad word right now. I stood at the wall looking at Helen, and I said, "She wasn't a mother to me in my eyes. And she was never a friend. She always said to me, I brought you into this world, so I can take you out of this world. I understand it's a common thing to say as a parent when upset, but her actions have shown me time and time again that it could actually happen. But God had other plans for me. You brought me here, so I owe you that, so let me repay you for your time."

I unzipped my track pants pockets and pulled the money out and said, "As I researched, it's $30- $40,000 to have a child." My godmother was now crying but I blocked her out. Nothing could distract me from what I came to do. So I took a step toward the table and said, "If you want to count it, you can. But, I know how much it is. I counted it myself and I've counted it more than once. It's $40,000. That's what it took for you to have me. So now you don't have anything over me. If you don't want to claim me as your daughter, that's also fine." Even though she never did that. Taking the next step to the table, I could hear the sound of the handcuffs in my head as I stepped towards the spot where I was arrested on my 16th birthday. All over money.

"As of today, you cannot say to me, 'I gave you life' because I'm paying you for it and the pain you felt, I feel it every week. We are even in my eyes.'" I put the money out, and outstretched my hand, but she didn't take it.

My godmother now with a hand on her forehead and crying was saying, "I can't believe this is what you're doing…" and I continued to block her out.

I kept on saying it over and over "You have nothing over me. And, that's how I want to live my life from today on, with nobody having nothing over me. If anyone in this room feels that I owe them something, do tell me now." I put the money on the table but I had to cross over my godmother.

She held my hand and she said, "You sure this is what you want to do?"

I pulled away from her gently and said, "Yes, you don't know how long it took me to get that money. I know what I'm doing."

I could feel my phone buzzing and my pager going. I caught a slight glimpse of the screen and saw that it was my dad calling me. Helen said, "I don't think this is right."

I quickly let her know, "It's not about you."

She said, "I want you guys to talk."

I responded to that with a smirk, "Money talks. And I'm going to walk away from this toxic mess today. It is done for me." My mother grabbed that money, went to the washroom, and I heard a flush. She did it because she had to prove a point. I told Helen, "I'll call you later." And she asked me to stay and talk to her. "I don't want to. I'll call you later, or I'll stop by the house tomorrow. Love you, bye."

I could see the disappointment in her eyes. But I could also see how she now knew that I was not the same girl that she raised. I was from the streets, I was not Claire Huxtable's daughter. I belonged to the streets. This is who I was. I was surprised she did not ask me, "Where did you get this money from?" To avoid her, I took the stairs and returned my dad's call. He was downstairs.

"What are you so happy about?" he asked. The look on my face gave its own answer. We drove and we said nothing. It was a short drive because I lived in the area. We just listened to music. Of course, by the time I got home, I had like 100 missed calls from my godmother. I turned off the phone. I did go see her the next day. She had company and I was glad because she wasn't going to have the conversation when she had company. I had a sandwich. I stayed there and I talked to my god brothers and sisters.

I then said, "Excuse me, I know you're busy with your guests. So I'll come back another day." She insisted that I stayed, but I said I'd be back.

I went to my room in her home. I've always had my room there. I lotioned my hands and then sat on my bed for five minutes. Going to Helen's, you have to dress differently. She didn't allow me to dress like a tomboy. She didn't allow me to wear tight clothes. I could never wear a t-shirt with any logos or words across my chest. I had on a pair of khaki slacks and a jeans top. I fed the pet birds they had in the house and then I left. She never asked me about the money again. I don't know why but she just asked me, "Where do you live again?" I just told her, "Yes, we still live in Mississauga."

I figured she was hearing something, but of course, I stuck to my story. Well, it was not really a lie, because my dad did have a room there and my mail went there... That whole year after whenever I saw my mother in passing, she would say, "Hi Kamelah, how are you?" She never said those things to me before. So I guess I gained her respect now.

I would always answer respectfully, "I'm good. How are you?" and keep it moving. Although seeing her triggered me, I had bigger things to deal with and would remember something.

My grandmother, my uncle, and my dad always said to me, "Blessed is a child that has their own. Remain humble – nothing happens before its time." For me, that was always in my mind. I practiced to always have my own stuff and what I didn't have, I would learn to do without. Even though I was once in a poor period of life, I did my best with what I had. Life is the best thing and you have another chance to make your situation better. In my mind, anything that didn't breathe life into me any longer, didn't weigh me down.

People started to call me British once my dad started living in the UK. He was still taking care of me even when he was outside of the country. He was paying my rent, buying me groceries, giving me lunch money and giving me money to get my hair done. He gave me anything I needed, as long as I completed school.

CHAPTER 4:

ART OF LIFE

That was what was on my mind the whole time. I could feel my phone buzzing a few times during the tour, and I knew that the caller could only be two people: the babysitter, or Frank. The babysitter I was more worried about but in this atmosphere, I didn't want to take my phone out.

As I got to the car, I looked at the call. It wasn't the babysitter, it was Frank. I called him back and he asked if everything was okay and when I was planning to go back to Toronto. I avoided his question and said, "I went to a museum."

He described the museum to me and asked, "Did you take the tour?! Did they give you the tour?!"

I said, "Calm down. I got a full tour, Harp gave me my own instructions on what I should do."

He just went on to say, "Well, you've got to go to this place, you've got to shop there, and you've got to see this. It's a very different experience. You're usually always locked into Jane & Finch, but this is like a whole new world. Things taste and feel different here."

"Ok," I said, "I get it, I hear you. I will be a tourist for you, Harp, her husband, and Richard at the Art Gallery. I will even go and buy a Montreal T-shirt and a map." Frank and I just laughed for a while. He went on to tell me that he really missed my company cause I always made him laugh.

He asked me, "How come you never ask me where I am?"

"Because it's not my business, if you wanted to tell me, you would have told me."

He said, ``I knew that would have been your answer."

I asked, "Well aren't you gonna tell me?" He just said no. So, I replied, "I didn't expect you to anyway. "

I asked him, "Are you going to ask me how much money it is?"

Again, he replied, "Nope. I never asked because I trust you. Whatever it is, I told you the Canadian currency you can take half of and I'll let you know what to do with the rest." He continued, and said, "You know, if you ever need to get a getaway, you could always stay at that apartment."

I told him I'm going to be driving now. Again, he just stayed on the phone on speaker saying nothing all the way back to the hotel. When I got to the hotel, I told him, "I know one person I was with would know your voice. I'm going to go upstairs with the girls and call you back later or we could correspond through text."

When I got into the lobby, a gentleman asked me, "Good evening. How was your day?"

I'm not used to people questioning me, but I put on a smile and replied, "FABULOUS!! I went out to eat, and had a few shopping trips." I was still holding onto the bag that Harp had given me. "I did a bit of sightseeing."

He said, "Oh, did you go to this place or that place?" The places he listed Harp had never mentioned so I wasn't interested.

I just replied to the gentleman, "No, I'll be looking at those tomorrow. THANKS FOR ASKING, HOW WAS YOURS?" In my head I'm asking myself, why is this man all up in my business?!

I turned to the front desk and asked, "Am I able to use the board room at any time?"

"Sure, absolutely," And he walked ME to the boardroom. I only went into the boardroom because I wanted to open the gift that Harp gave me. There was a box that I had noticed before. In the box there was a charm. There was no bracelet for the charm. The charm was a moon. Behind the moon, there was an engraving. On one side of the moon was the American $100 bill and the other side of the moon was just smooth.

The box also had a clasp for the charm and the paperwork for it. The paperwork stated which jewelry store the charm was bought from and that it was 18 karat gold. I removed the remaining tissue paper and there was an envelope. I opened the card; it was a thank you card but it was velvet.

The card also said, "Frank speaks so highly of you. This is my gift for your trip." In the envelope there were just $100 bills.

I sat back in the chair and I'm like, "Do I dare count it?" I took a moment - it was $2,500 in just $100 bills. I don't know if Harp thought I needed it or it was just a random gift or just her being nice as the card said. I don't know what kind of transaction took place between Frank and Harp. I never asked. I just sat in the boardroom for a little bit of time and then I went upstairs to my friends. I acted like the past few hours were nothing. When they asked me where I was, I told them I went to meet a friend.

They were questioning if we were going to go out tonight, so I told them they were free to go out. "I don't drink, I don't smoke, so you guys can go and have a good time.

They said, "We're not leaving you." Of course, they packed for the occasion of going out; I didn't. But, I had a pair of jeans sneakers and a top that had a dressy vibe to it. We went out on the town of Montreal.

On our way back to Toronto, I said, "Do you guys want to do some sightseeing?" They agreed and I mentioned how the other day, someone told me we should go to this museum. One of my friends was saying that the hotel staff had been asking them if they had gone to any of the museums or had done any sightseeing. Everyone was down to go. I just reminded them to act right.

We stopped at this museum. Unfortunately, it was closed. There were some staff leaving and they reminded us of their business hours. I told them, "Well, we're on our way back to Toronto. It's just what my friend Harp said..." Again, the demeanor changed, the doors opened, the lights went on.

They said, "Well, we can't give you the full tour. I know that Harp would be disappointed, but we can just show you around the main hall." The employee went on to describe some of the art sculptures and art pieces. I was shocked that my friends were interested, because they're so hood. They were all in complete awe. The attendant was explaining the pieces, who made them, and where they were from. We were there for probably just 10 minutes because it was closing time.

I suggested to them, "Okay let's go."

The attendant assured us, "No, no, no. You can stay."

While leaving she said, " Is it possible that you can do me a favor and not tell Harp that I never gave you the full tour?"

"Oh absolutely. That's fine," I said. "We don't even live here and you have done more than enough for us."

She continued, "I know I should have given you the full tour, but I have my small kids to go home to and the other staff weren't here when I let you guys in. "

I told her, "That's fine, I totally understand and we appreciate what you did for us."

So, we drove back to Toronto. When getting back into the city, I called Frank and he asked if the drive home was safe. He could just hear my friends in the background carrying on and on about all the things we did for the couple of days we were there. I stepped away and I said to him, "What's next? Because you know, I have school and I have things to do."

He said, "Well, what do you want to do next?"

I said to him, "To be honest, I'm tired. and you know I don't like to drive."

He just said, "Okay, I'll call you tomorrow and we'll get into it. There's a lot to get done. What you saw was just a few months of work that I did. So, you make the decision if you want that to be the rest of your life." I told him bluntly I can't answer that right now and we can talk in 3 days. I needed to spend time with my kids and study and rest my mind.

With the money from Harp, I paid some bills, but I still didn't know what to do with the half of the money that Frank said to take. Some months had passed, and I had traveled to the States and to Jamaica. Throughout all my travels, I did not take my cell phone. So, when I got back to Canada, I had a lot of missed calls from Frank. When I called him back, I didn't get an answer. Even when I tried to reach him by text there was no response. I didn't know if I should go to the apartment because I wasn't getting a response from him at all.

I had graduation coming up for my college course for computers, and my dad had also got himself in a little bit of trouble. Which led me to make a decision. I would use some of this money to help him out. I didn't know if I should use the rest of the money to invest in myself or, continue to just wait and tell not a soul. My choice was to tell no one, I still acted like every day was the day before I opened that door because I was still doing some other stuff. The offer that he gave me was still on the table whenever he came back or called to advise me what to do. I would deal with that decision then. So, I went on about my life; I completed school and completed graduation.

Where I was living the old man Mario had passed away and his daughter had come to the unit and announced his passing. She wanted us out of the unit, which was fine. She was a bit rude about it but the stern look I gave her calmed her down real fast. I put in an application to move from one building to the next. That new building was more of a party building. A lot of people from the area lived in it. From the first 1st floor, right up to the 19th floor, I knew basically 50% of the building. This had its pros and cons - as in, it would have more of a cover up if I needed it along with some company, if and when I got bored. However, there were way too many people to maneuver around to keep my business at an all time low but that was a challenge that I was willing to overcome.

The young lady that I had stayed with at this point was someone that I knew from the area before I moved out of the condo. She made a statement to me that will stay with me for the rest of my life. One day she told me, "I'm not your friend like that. I'm only your friend for what you can do for me." People around me were upset, but to this day, I'm not upset with Ashley, to this day, because she was always straightforward.

Most people would act as if they liked me or had my best interests in a friendship at heart. To me, I had to rate her for that. Ashley had moved to the other building before me. I had two units at a time. While moving back and forth, I still had two months to move out of the condo and was fixing up the new unit in the other building. I saw Ashley one day in the lobby, not knowing she had moved back home. I thought she had moved back home, but she had actually moved in with some friends of mine.

This was surprising to me because when Ashley was with me, she didn't have money for rent. She didn't have any money to put towards groceries, toiletries or bus fare. She didn't explain to me that she was moving in with my friend. She explained to me she was going back home to her mother. Although she was blunt about her reasoning this opened my eyes to someone who's so transparent and bold, you have to have your guard up just as the next person or even more.

As they say, "Keep your friends and their bold-ass enemies closer." Our building was a hot-spot on Fridays and Saturdays. All of us attended parties, and my house became somewhat of a hang out spot for a few of us. The building became a place of unity where there were mad life plans. We had good times, fights, arguments, and good cries for our fallen friends.

There were a set of twins that I knew from my childhood. Alana also lived on the same floor as me. My god sister Brina also lived with me; she made me feel more safe and she brought a sense of security and peace of mind. She was the type to listen and speak justice without judging. She made my sad moments joyful with just a few words. We often did each other's hair, cooked and hung out with the others. Overall, we were a combo of fun and badness. After a few months in this building, I became someone who knew how to get things.

I denied it at times, but a few people already knew some things from a few years before that I had helped them with, and when they needed help again or for family, they would turn to me. I still maintained the whole, "I know someone that knows someone" routine. I wasn't about to paint a picture of me being the plug.

Paperwork became a side hustle for me, along with boosting mostly for myself and kids. I then started to make sales. It was risky, but also a good cover up for my spending. So I would go on the road from time to time getting clothes, shoes, accessories and handbags weekly. I soon became the, "If you need clothes for a good price, you can get it from me" person.

Brina was pregnant at the time so I would go out and get stuff for the baby. She stayed with me for a period of time until she had her baby who became my goddaughter. She was not short of anything and the guys that we hung out with gave the baby so much as well. I would love getting to sit down with them and have deep conversations about pastimes in Jamaica. Brina was very close to my family as well. She never knew it but she was my personal therapist.

People would try to come between Brina and I. It reminded me time and time again why I was never one for a lot of female company. It wasn't working out for me. In my mind I thought, "How am I going to take myself away without hurting them?" I think that's a part of me being a more nurturing person. Since childhood, I'd come to nurture people and their needs and feelings before mine. That did not last too long though. I was still not hearing from Frank, still not going to the apartment, and still not touching the money - even though half was mine.

I did become a bit worried from time to time with so many people around me dying. I also started to lose a lot of friends as they became envious. Their envy began to divide me from some of them. At first, I was angry, but soon after I became wiser. I had been trying to figure out a way to drop half of these friends anyway - the handouts were becoming annoying. A trip to Jamaica settled my decision. While I was in Jamaica, I learned a friend that would come by was there prior to my arrival. When I got to Jamaica, I was approached by a few gentlemen who said, "Your friend stole our stuff, and you introduced us to her." I said to them, "I don't know what you're talking about. And, I don't know who you're talking about. Explain yourself, because I can see your anger." They responded to me saying, "If it wasn't for your father, we would kill you."

CHAPTER 5:

FAMILY, RESPECT & TRAVELS

I could see the situation was getting pretty serious. So, they went on to explain to me who they were speaking about and what was stolen from them. I said, "You know, to be honest, I no longer speak with that person."

The one with the rough voice cut me off to say, "At the end of the day, we want our stuff back. Is there any way you could try and get it back for us?" I was in shock with his tone. Before I would have never guessed he wanted me to do him a favor.

"What would you want me to do? I don't speak to her. I don't know where she is in Canada. If she's not answering your phone calls all I can do is try giving her a call." Well, I called the wrong number. Anyway, that was never my business, and I didn't want to get involved.

I went on my cell phone and I dialed some random numbers. I didn't know who would answer it then but I knew it wouldn't have been her. I put the phone on speaker and of course, there was an Asian lady who answered and I just hung up the phone. A few of the younger ones in their 20s had the most attitude, but I could see that they were trying to work too hard because they kept looking over at the older people that were there. Not all of them were engaging in the conversation. They were playing cards and cooking on an outside fire. "Well Kam Kam, could you do something for us?"

I said, "What is it exactly that you would like me to do?"

They said, "We need the situation to get fixed. We're broke, and we need it to get dealt with. When are you leaving Jamaica?"

Oh, of course I lied and said, "I'll be leaving Jamaica in a week." But my trip was really ending in three weeks.

The tall one said, "We can get it together for you in one week."

I asked, "What is it exactly that you guys are getting together?" They said drugs.

I laughed not giving a damn how bad they thought they were or how mad they were and said, "You gotta be kidding me."

They told me, "Your friend stole from us and it was a quantity of drugs." I didn't know her to be that type of person. I continued to listen and chuckle at the same time. They explained to me that she'd been doing this for quite some time. That explained why I wasn't seeing her so often. We never had an argument or falling out, we just stopped seeing each other. She stopped coming around.

I could tell she had leveled up, but I was just happy that she did. This was the furthest thing from my mind. However, I wasn't about to give them that explanation. Just from the look on my face, they knew that I had no clue what was going on. I told them bluntly, "There are many things that cross my mind daily and I dismiss them all quickly and there are a lot of things I don't put my hands on. My friends would be one of them. Furthermore, I find it to be disrespectful that you would come to me with this offer - knowing who my father is."

They got defensive and said, "We just asked Kam Kam nah mek it look so we don't wah you a do it. True, you come down here so often we did think…"

The old one stopped him and went on to say, "We just wanted to know if you could help us find her, if you made the call and did not get her, let it go. When you go back home, if you see her, let her know everything is good. I will tek this loss for now. But don't tell the elder (my dad) about this, everything bless."

I saw that they had respect when it came to my dad. Well, did he get through to the younger ones and said low dat or go home? I heard one of them ask. "Really now? A who da BITCH YAH?" while walking off. I was not having it at all. I might have been from Canada but I was far from a punk… I started off with a screw face and said, "Bitch like your grandmother that swallowed sperm and got pregnant by accident to have your mother who had a hungry half dead looking disrespectful piece a shit by her uncle…"

We immediately got into a heated argument. Now other people in that community heard what was going on, but not in detail. I noticed us drawing some attention, which led me to come away from the argument. The old folks and his friends told him to stop as it did not look good to fight with a girl. He just expected me to clap back so fast with words that cut deep. He was still going at it while walking up the road. Fair enough, I would not be the one to tell my dad now - someone would.

When I returned to Canada, I inquired as to where my old friend was just to know if she was ok. Sheila was way younger than I was and she had entered something that was way bigger than her. Some time had passed, but this situation still weighed heavy on my mind. I came to find out that this young girl basically threw away her life to do this, as I had found out that she had been taken to jail on another small island and these people never helped her.

It gave me a reality check that no matter how much they respected my parents, that could have been me if I did not stand up on my own feet. Not all money is good money - what they pay you you can't even pay for a lawyer. It's either you do your time or turn into a rat and we all know that's not going to go well. Even though I was around drugs growing up, I washed my hands from it. I've seen good people die or lose family, friends, homes and respect from their community. I also saw a lot of people come back from bad drug habits - but that's their story to tell.

At this time, I began to lose a lot of my friends to crime and murder. I found myself going to funerals more than I was going to parties. One particular year, I wore the same two funeral outfits, basically every other weekend. It got bad enough to the point where I stopped going. I just made up my mind that I would not be attending any more funerals. I thought I should be attending more weddings. At one of the funerals when I made this decision, I saw Sheila. I could tell that she was avoiding me.

So I walked up to her and I said, "Are you okay? Where have you been?" Of course, she lied and said that she was okay. She was going to school out of the city.

So I sternly grabbed her by the hand, not that anybody would notice, and I told her, "What you're doing is not worth it. What they're paying you, the money is not worth it unless you're working for yourself to invest in your future self. You have a lot of years ahead of you. Buy clothes that will only last for the season, put your money to use please." I could see the tears welling up in her eyes, but because she already lied, I wasn't up for it. I wasn't pleased with it but I spoke my mind, let go of her hand slowly and walked away from her. That was the end of our friendship or whatever we were at the time - it died at that funeral.

I was drawn to my friend Kelly more than the rest. She had this little red car we would go on the road with. What I liked about going outside with her was that it was intimate. Our conversations were for the future; our world debates and her random thoughts out of nowhere and that habit she had of always getting to the end of a story ahead of time... We would sing, dress up and go out to eat, and we lived a classy boosting life when we were together. That relationship lasted to this day. Even though she had her other company, when we were together, it was like a bond, but specifically, a bond of our minds.

She would express the respect she had for me and she would see through me. She would always say to me, "I don't know why you let people perceive you to be this mean girl. If people really knew you, they would know that you're silly, you're fun, and you're compassionate." I used to tell her that I don't like to show that. She would encourage me, "You should start to show that side of you." I would explain to her in detail that I didn't want anyone to know my weaknesses.

The way I'd cope with the rest of the world was through that of ambiguity. If people wanted to speculate, that was fine by me. I didn't want to give them that piece of information on how to get me down, and she understood. We went on to make a lot of money together. She's a better saver than I am and she's very simple; even though we will treat ourselves to luxurious things.

On a bi-monthly basis, she would like to partner. A partner is where we would save money, whether it was $100 or $200 a week, and at the end of 30 days, 90 days, or a year, we would collect all that money. I would give her my partner money weekly. Again, she was really good at saving and I always joked with her that she should be an accountant.

She would travel to Jamaica often as well. There were times when we weren't together. I found that the times that we weren't together, it made me very strong. I mean strong as in I didn't get that time to be at ease. So, I put up this wall against the world even though I had my other friends, my guard was always up. It was a bit draining, but it worked.

Where we lived, there was a little hill and on that hill, there was a group of young men that used to hang out there. Most, if not all of them, knew my dad. I was still just a little girl to them. I would pass by daily and hang out with them for a half hour or so. Of course, the majority of them were drug dealers. The rest of them were just hanging out and their girlfriends stood by them while dealing. They were a crew of well-dressed young men. They were always just respectful and sometimes they would even say, "We don't even know why you hang out with us. You don't drink, you don't smoke, and I'm not about to explain anything to your dad if something should happen." I had a cousin that was there and he would not let anything happen to me. Their conversations were intriguing with the way they would be speaking about their hustling ways.

Any conversation when it was about money or business always intrigued me. I would hang out with them just to see if I could apply their world of life to what I was doing. They had no idea what I was doing with fraud or boosting. However, there were many lessons learned on that hill, and I admired their unity.

Most of these gentlemen ended up going to jail, while some of them had faded away from the community to start their families. It crossed my mind that they didn't have jobs, yet they would drive luxurious cars and dress nice daily. It was confusing to me that they didn't see their image as the reason why they kept getting into trouble. But I never voiced that to them, I just kept it to myself. Even though most of what they did was crime - out of those crime conversations came good life lessons, customer service situations, and good business strategies.

I ended up graduating from computer college. I invited no one to my graduation - I just went on to collect my diploma then went and got something to eat at a restaurant. I came home like it never happened. I would have days where I was starting to get flashbacks of the murder of my friend's mom, my dad being arrested, or my friends' funerals. This soon caused me to shut down and distance myself.

In that time of shutting down, I basically wrote out a master plan for the money that Frank gave to me. Basically, a whole year had passed. My kids were getting bigger. My dad had now migrated to the UK. So, I had to stand firm for myself.

I received a phone call early one morning from a schoolmate of mine but they were calling from jail. So I asked, "How are you? And one, how did you get my number? And two, if you're in jail, how do you have a phone?"

Their response was simple, "Frank gave me your number and having a phone where I am is nothing."

I asked, "Frank gave you my number? Where's Frank?"

He said, "I don't know, I just know that I got a number to give to you to call Frank."

After putting the number in my other phone, we continued on to just have a simple conversation . "How are you? How are you doing? How's so and so?" And that was that. Our conversation lasted a whole 4 minutes.

I never heard back from that person ever again. I didn't call Frank immediately. I had my nephew staying with me from Jamaica at this time and my hands were full. At this point I knew that calling him back would lead me into something and I did not have the time for that. I was on the verge of medical school. I needed a few advanced credits in science and math so I registered for night school. I was still in the game; still boosting, and doing a little bit of fraud work. So, I had my own money and I kind of had blocked Frank's situation out of my mind. Thus, I was hesitant to give him that phone call.

I took a trip back to Montreal and I visited Harp. Unexpectedly, she greeted me with the same open arms and as I walked into the house, we went to a different sitting room this time. Everything in this room was white and gold. She said, "Nobody really sits in this room because it's pure white, but I had a feeling that the conversation that we're going to have is going to be pure, so we can sit here."

Harp and I sat in that room for over three hours. She was humming and I was just relaxed in her loveseat. Then she asked, "What is it that you're thinking? Is it long term or short term?" I didn't have an answer at first, because I really had to think about it. In my mind, at the time, there was hurt, anger, revenge, and confusion. I would often be trying to plan for the future, but the plans that I had were being stopped by all of these emotions. Harp was a different type of lady. For her to even ask me that, it kind of opened my eyes. I had elders to speak to, I could have always also gone to my godmother.

However, I just chose to take this road trip. She asked me what I wanted for supper. I told her that I wasn't really that hungry and that I just wanted a cup of tea. She made me some lemon and honey tea. Then she said, "Let's go upstairs." We went upstairs where she had a library. She told me to sit at a desk. It was a big cherrywood desk and there were books everywhere around me. She said, "Sit here for as long as you want. Whatever decision that you make, think about it twice. Don't let the money be a part of your plan."

To this day, I take that statement seriously. I sat there and then I just told her, "Okay, I'm going home."

She said, "You took all this time, you can't go home. You're going to drive all the way back to Toronto?" I told her yes, I just needed to get away for some time. My kids were with a friend of mine and I just wanted to go home. She then came to me with a bag in her hand.

I said, "No Harp, not this time. I'm okay. I already know your tricks and trades, it's okay."

She said to me, "You know, my door is always open for you." Harp and her husband greeted me off and I just drove back to Toronto with my thoughts and my new plan.

Part of that new plan was that I needed a better cover up. This better cover everything up or I had to give it all up. I took medical administration and blood lab tech courses. I never missed a day of school, not one day. I took a night study group once a week just so I didn't fail. Failing was not part of the plan.

While going to college , I spoke to Frank once. He just asked me questions:

"Did you go to the apartment?"

"Absolutely not."

"Are you upset with me?"

"Absolutely not."

"Did you spend your money yet?"

"Absolutely not."

Then I asked him, "Are you coming back to the city?"

He said, "Absolutely not."

"What are you going to do with that apartment?"

He said, "You don't have to worry about that apartment. I just want to know that you're okay. What do you want to do? I want to make sure that you're alright."

I said, "You know, you're younger than I am. You don't have to worry about me so much."

"Yes, I do. You're too smart. I don't want you to get lost in what you're doing. I heard that you're going to school. I like that road for you but as you said I'm younger than you. I can't tell you what to do." He laughed, "I just want you to know that if you ever need a place to stay and clear your mind, you can always go to the unit. Nobody knows about it. You can do this rather than driving all the way to Montreal and back in one day."

We stayed on the phone for probably like 10 or 15 minutes and then I didn't speak to Frank for probably the next six months. In those six months, I had an encounter with a schoolmate from middle school. I met her when I was at a big wholesale grocery store. She remembered me by the scar that I had over my eye. She said, "Kamelah?!" Mind you, I don't really answer to my real name in public. I was startled, but I never turned to see who said my name, but then she tapped me on the shoulder.

CHAPTER 6:

KIND TROUBLES

That tap was a trigger for me because I was a booster. It's something security or floor walkers (or undercover security as we called them) would do. But, I was buying groceries for the kids so it didn't startle me as much. She said to me, "Kamelah, how are you?"

I turned to her, "Hi Trina, how are you doing? How did you remember me?"

She explained that she remembered my face with the scar over my forehead and, "That walk you got is strong."

I said to her, "Are you okay?" I could see that she looked wild in her eyes. Her eyes were really glossy, and she was very shaky.

She said, "No, not really. Why do you ask?" I stated it was just out of concern.

She had a little bag of groceries in her hand, and I questioned, "That's all that you're buying, five items in this big wholesale store?"

She didn't answer so I said, "Put it in my cart, it's okay." I ended up paying for her five items. My wholesale bill that day was $500.

She followed me to my car. Just by walking with her, I could tell something was wrong. She helped me pack my items into my car and she said, "Do you still live in Jane and Finch?"

I said, "Yeah, why? You've been there lately?"

"No. I just got back to the city" she said slowly. I asked where she had been and she said, "Oh, I was out in Barrie for some time."

I said, "Oh, Barrie's a nice place."

She said, "No, it's not!" and suddenly began to cry.

Trina was a beautiful girl - slim thick, with amazing, shapely hips and a small waist. She was mixed with white and black and she had one of a kind green eyes. We were in the middle of the parking lot and there was a fair-skinned girl crying profusely. I'm like, "Okay go in the car because I don't want anyone to think that I did anything to you." We sat in the car and she just began to say that she was on drugs and that she ran away from her pimp, AND she was pregnant. In my head I'm thinking, Oh my god! Another problem that I couldn't solve. Why me?!

I asked her, "What kind of drugs are you on?" She said pills, heroine, and that she smoked weed. She had been wearing a cardigan and when she took it off, her arms were destroyed. She had bruises everywhere. She said, "I'm not here alone."

I said, "What does that mean? Did you have kids before?" Who could be with her?

She responded, "There's six of us."

"Six of who - of who?!"

She explained, "It's me and my friends."

"Well, where are they?"

The wholesale store was in a plaza and she told me the other girls were in other stores in the plaza.

She explained, "We all ran away." Meaning, they all ran away from this sex trade lifestyle that they were living. One of the girls had her son with her. He was about 3 years old.

I said, "Trina, okay, if you never saw me, what were you going to do?"

She said, "Well, I was going to steal the food and just sell myself until I got enough money to stay somewhere."

With confusion I said, "Six of you...YOU make seven, add a child makes eight. You guys had no plan?"

She said, "Well some of the girls are from Nova Scotia, some of the girls are from Barrie and some of the girls are Haitian."

I said, "Trina I can give you guys some money," and her eyes lit up. There was something in my mind saying, let them stay at the apartment, but I couldn't have them all stay there, that would be too many people in that apartment. Further, I didn't even put everything in place yet. I said, "Okay Trina, I have some money I can give you. There's a local motel. It's in the outside corridors of Jane and Finch. I can't drive all of you, my car is already full of groceries. I'll call a cab. You can come with me. The girl with the child can come with us in my car." I called the cab and waited and we went to the motel. I just told her that I would be paying for the rooms, but some of the girls would have to share.

"I'm just doing this for two weeks. You guys have to figure it out after. This is way too much for me. But I'll pay for it." I gave them some of the groceries from the car. They thanked me, they were happy and they were pleased. I took Trina and the girl with her son aside and said, "You know you guys didn't just come to Toronto with no plan. I find that hard to believe. I'm not telling you what to do, but I did not pay for you to continue to sell yourself while you're here. Trina, you came from a good family. How did you end up in this situation?"

"My dad is the one who put me on drugs. During high school, I was sexually assaulted. So, this is all that I know. I don't have a trade; I didn't finish high school. I barely passed middle school to go to high school."

The girl with the son was also mixed. I asked her, "Okay where's the child's father?" Just in the moment, I had so many questions on my mind trying to understand how they got into this mess. I didn't even give her time to answer. I got having to do what you had to do just to stay alive but for me, this was a different lifestyle right in front of my eyes. I continued to ask her, "Why do you have your son with you?"

She said, "Well, this is how I provide for him and I'd rather have him with me than end up in the system." I was just in a state of confusion and a bit of anger. I was just flustered with the whole situation and it was getting late. I had groceries that were starting to melt. I told Trina I would check up on her in a few days and that she could call me if she needed to.

I couldn't stand the drive home from the motel. The stench that was left in my car was unbearable. I just had to say to myself, Is this part of my plan? Like, this is taking away from what I need to do. I went home and I thought about it in depth. Should I let Trina stay at this apartment? I wondered. It had been there for years now and it was not being used. This young girl had a child and a motel was not a place for a child. On the other hand, their lifestyle would bring so much attention to that unit. I couldn't have that. This situation continued to weigh heavy on my mind.

Trina called me the next morning. I could hear in the background these women were just thanking me and they seemed to be doing okay. Later that day I dropped $300 off for them just to get some food and some necessities. I had brought a pizza too. I had no idea what they liked but one cannot go wrong with pizza. Even though Trina was the one I really know, I was intrigued with this young girl and her young baby. "You guys have to come up with a plan." I didn't really have a lot of conversation with the other girls other than just saying hi or goodbye.

Three weeks into this situation, I made a decision to have Trina and the girl with the son stay at that unit. It was a safe environment; they could get themselves cleaned up or whatever. I mean, I just had to go there, take up what I needed to get and put it in storage and that was my plan. I called Trina that afternoon and I told her the plan. I told her that I was going to come by and that I was going to talk to her and her friend with the son. She said, "You didn't get my message?"

I said, "No. I don't really check messages. What's up?" She said some of the girls had gone back and Candy, the girl with her son, was still with Trina. Trina also warned me that Candy was taking a lot of drugs.

I said to Trina, "I don't understand this lifestyle and you guys got to get it together because what I'm telling you is that I don't want this at the place where you have a baby on the way. This is a good example of what not to do. I'll talk to you guys tomorrow." I got upset; I didn't know what to do differently and I had to rethink things. I couldn't have Candy there doing drugs and doing it around her son.

Trina went on to say, "No, I will keep her baby."

I asked her, "You're not taking drugs too are you?" She said, "Not as much." I got angry and I hung up the phone.

I didn't hear from Trina the next day. I had a module mock exam that I was studying for. My phone wouldn't stop buzzing in my pocket during the testing time, to the point where my teacher said to me, "I remember you have children, do you think it's your children calling you?" I told her, "Miss, I really don't know." "Okay, um pass me your test and step out and answer it. You got 2 minutes. If it's not the children just come back. Better yet, let's just, everybody pass me your tests and let's all take a five-minute break." Some of my classmates were annoyed, others were happy that they could take a cigarette break.

I didn't know the phone number that had been contacting me. I got texts saying over and over "SOS. SOS, 911, 911." So I thought to myself, who the heck is this? What the heck are they doing blowing up my phone? I went to the vending machine and I got a bag of chips and orange juice. My phone vibrated again, this time I answered it and I said "Hello?" The person on the other end of the line was just crying, almost screaming. I'm like, "Okay, who is this and what is it?"

All they could mutter was, "…Trina…" And I knew something was wrong. "She's…she's not moving…she, she's not moving…" That's all she said over and over again.

Candy (the young one with the son) had overdosed and was in the hospital and Trina had also passed away from an overdose. I didn't even ask who the caller was, I guessed it may have been one of the girls that had already gone back to Barrie. This person went on to warn me, "The police are looking for you."

I said, "For what?!,"

"Well, the man at the motel thinks that you're their pimp." You've got to be kidding me. She explained, "He gave the police a full description of you and your car."

I said, "How do you know this?"

"Well, one of the girls had to work out of the motel. She didn't go back to Barrie, she was still there. She called me and told me, ``I had been calling you to tell you."

I got so upset. "You've got to be kidding me like, are you high? You've gotta be lying. You've got to be kidding me. A pimp?! As a woman? What is that?!"

I walked back into the exam room; I finished the test. I turned off my phone, which was something I didn't do often. When I walked out of school, I turned on my phone. There were so many missed calls. Upon driving to my building and seeing the amount of police, I knew it was for me. Of course, the police stopped me and asked if I was Kamelah and if I knew Trina Lamtom. I said yes to my name, and nothing else.

They brought me in for questioning. I called my lawyer, of course. A pimp?! I found it funny but in the same breath, I was grieving my friend I had known from middle school through to high school. This happened in less than a month from meeting Trina at the wholesale store. My friend was dead and they thought I was her pimp?!There was a kid with them and I didnt even know Candy. My lawyer was driving to the station. "Well, this is what it looks like."

I said, "But, what it looks like is not what it is. I don't know the first thing about being a pimp."

I was at the police station for hours. Nobody knew what was going on. I told my lawyer to call the babysitter and tell her I ran into a bit of trouble but that I was ok. She probably thought it was for boosting or whatever, but it wasn't. My lawyer came down for a couple of hours. My lawyer turned to me and said, "This doesn't look good for you. You paid for their rooms and there's footage of these girls with you handing them money and another with you having an argument with them. How do you know them?" "I didn't want to have this conversation. What do you mean my friend died?" He was like, "She died of a heroin overdose."

My lawyer turned to me and said, "How do you plan on getting out of this situation? It doesn't look good."

I said, "I don't know, what am I supposed to prove?"

He said, "They have her cell phone. She called you and another person only. Part of your text messages is saying "Yes, I'm going to bring you money. Yes, I'm going to bring you some groceries." It's hard not to say you're not their pimp when they have a long rap sheet for prostitution." To be honest, we just sat in that room.

All I could say to him over and over was, "This was never part of my plan. It wasn't part of the plan… and this was going to cost me a lot to get out of."

Like I said, this all happened in under 30 days of me reconnecting with Trina. I was trying so hard to process it all. "What do you mean my pregnant friend was dead? What do you mean I'm being charged for human trafficking? Are you kidding me?!" Candy was in the hospital for some period of time. I'm not sure who had her child. My lawyers said, "Let's question Candy." The lawyers took advantage of Candy being in the hospital. This way they knew where to find her. There was another girl who they questioned - the same one that called me on the day of the incident. Eventually, she stopped answering her phone, and I don't blame her.

Candy told my lawyer that she met me at the wholesale store and that I was most definitely not her pimp or a pimp at all. She went into details about how nice I was to her and her son. He asked, "How did Kamelah transport you to the motel?" She explained that I called a taxi and she came with me. My lawyer contacted the Taxi company, and one of the taxi drivers was Haitian. One of the girls I had helped was also Haitian and he explained to my lawyer how he and the woman had a conversation during their ride to the hotel. The girl I helped explained to him that she didn't even know who I was and that she was actually thanking God that she could get a place to stay and something to eat. So, the Haitian taxi driver was a witness for me.

He then got that girl to come back and give her statement, "I don't know her, but she was basically our savior for 2-3 weeks. I went back because the way she talked to us was so stern. I didn't want to disappoint her, so I went to Vancouver and started a nail-tech program." I ended up with those witnesses. The motel owner on the other hand, was a complete jackass because he saw me as a pimp for whatever reason and what he witnessed.

My lawyer asked him, "Does this happen a lot at your motel?"

That jackass replied, "What do you mean does this happen a lot? It's a motel…" He wasn't the best witness. We also got footage from the wholesale store on the day I met Trina. So, the court had seen from the footage that when I met up with Trina, she already had stuff in her bag to steal before I got there, then the footage showed when she tapped me on the shoulder and I offered to pay for the groceries she had. There was an outside camera too so the wholesale store had the footage when she was helping me with my groceries and of her crying. They couldn't really see her face and her tears, but on camera you could definitely see her shoulders hunched over like she was sobbing and me rubbing her back. The next thing that the footage showed was the taxi driving up to the wholesale. The footage had replayed basically what I had been saying had happened from the get go. So the charges against me didn't last.

Trina's mom had been calling me. She actually wanted to meet up with me. I told her that I wasn't up for it, and she offered, "If there's anything that you ever need, you can call and let me know." She was going through her own grieving process and I was going through my own process now too. I was still losing friends and I had promised myself that I didn't want to go to any more funerals. Still, I did drive to Barrie and I did attend Trina's funeral. A lot of the girls that were there with us that day at the wholesale store, were there.

As they saw me, they hugged me. You could tell that they were sad, but you could feel the love in the room regardless of their lifestyles. She was loved. Trina had a big family. I stepped out before the service was almost over. It had become a routine for me, as I knew what would happen next. They were gonna roll the casket by and I didn't feel that I wanted to do that. I didn't want to be so close to her casket.

When I was leaving, one of the girls asked, "Why are you leaving?"

I said, "No, I'm just stepping out for a moment."

"Oh, thank you for going outside, I'm in need of some fresh air. Are you going to have a smoke?" I kindly let her know that I didn't smoke. Coming down the church steps, I looked back. It was a nice church. When I went outside, there was a group of men. I was wearing black slacks, black heels, and my big brim hat, with a lace blouse. They greeted me, "Hey Ma!"

I responded, "Hi good morning, how are you?" I had to tip my head back for them to see me underneath the hat.

I guess my response wasn't a typical response for them. They said "You're not from around here."

I said, "No I'm not."

"So how do you know Trina?"

"She's a school friend of mine. How do you know her?"

One of the men piped up, "That's my lady." I asked, "What do you mean? She's your girlfriend?" He never said that he was her pimp, but he and his friends laughed at my questions. I did not remember that I was at a church. I just felt myself getting hot.

I cursed him out with the church door behind me. I gave him every swear word in English and Patois to the point where I was sweating. He was giving it back to me - until he saw that I was really serious. His friends tried to calm me down. I was trying not to be loud as the girls were sitting at the church doors. I guess they figured out from my behavior that I was the girl from Toronto as one of them said, "She's from Jane and Finch."

I went on to say to him, with my teeth clenched, "I shouldn't be getting arrested for your guys' dirty line of work. And how dare you come here and proudly say you're a pimp with pride, knowing you're part of the reason she's gone?!" I didn't realize I was crying as I was just so angry and livid. If this was Toronto, I would have punched him in the face, but feelings have no boundaries, and so I punched him in the jaw. A few of the guys pulled me away quickly.

"We understand you're upset…" They wanted to explain to me.

One of the guys took me aside and said, "You have to understand, some people sell flowers on the street side, others sell drugs, and a few people sell themselves. The good, bad and the ugly are on one corner and they all have their customers. We never put Trina on drugs."

I tried to calm down. He said, "Wipe your tears." Then I realized I was crying. "You know that nobody talks to us like this."

I said, "I don't give a…" There he cut me off real quick. "You know what your intentions for the girls were and I respect that." He actually thanked me. "I was brought into this life, my dad was a pimp and this is the only life that I know. Sometimes, I let my girls have their own money but I don't tell the guys. So I understand your pain. I'm actually trying to get out of it. When the girls told me what you did, it actually gave me the strength to think I could walk away." The way he looked at me, it was like he looked through me. "Thank you," he said. "You don't know me but you opened my eyes to see that I can do better and that I don't need this lifestyle. This lifestyle hurts people. It hurts their families. Like look at where we are. We're at a funeral. If there were more people like you… and you've got a strong right hook…" We both laughed.

Then he hugged me. The way he hugged me brought me back to that moment, in that bedroom when I held my two friends as their mom died. This man held me so tight that it felt like our bones connected.

Trina's casket had passed. I didn't even realize it until people started walking past us and getting into their cars - there were so many. We made our way to the cemetery. When we arrived, I stayed far away. I didn't like to hear the sound of the dirt hitting the casket, it triggered me. That same gentleman stood by me. "I'm Alex by the way," he said. "Nice to meet you again," I bluffed. "I'm Kristine."

I went to the reception but I didn't stay long. The food spread was amazing! It was a mix of Italian food, Jamaican and Caribbean food and they had a live band perform. There were people there from all walks of life. I said my goodbyes to the parents and drove home with Alex on my mind. Just his words… they were so chilling that they echoed in my brain the whole way home. Barrie is not that far from Toronto but it still felt like quite a drive in my mind. It felt like a two-hour drive.

I just had a feeling of overwhelming peace from Trina's funeral. It was just a sincere moment driving home that I had done well, even in that situation. It was a tough situation that she was running from. It was an even tougher situation that she died from. But, if that young gentleman changed his life because of the situation, then it was well.

CHAPTER 7:

SAY A PRAYER OR TWO

With both of my parents now out of the country and my mother's side of the family still thinking of me as a black sheep, I didn't really have any desire to be around them. Oftentimes, they would invite me to places - whether it be Thanksgiving get-togethers , birthdays, family reunions, or Christmases. I used to go by my aunt's, my mother's sister, for Christmas dinner every so often. While I was there, they would speak ill of my mother. I didn't really like it. Then they began to bring up things, old things about my dad or things that they assumed about me and my brothers and my sisters, saying that we wouldn't amount to anything.

It was like they got joy or Chris Cringle out of negativity and false news. I knew they wanted a reaction about it so my only response was, "Did you tell her how you feel because she is not here and I can't answer for her." When it came to my dad, I just said, "Would you like me to call him and tell him?" I couldn't help it, but I laughed and the adults in the room got upset. But I kept on laughing.

The following Christmas, let's just say I had a plan for holiday cheer. I attended Christmas dinner and everybody got a gift. One of the things that my grandmother had said the previous year was that I was like my mom and all I knew how to do was steal and be dishonest. Her side of the family were all people of faith and active church-goers. I never once denied that I was a booster. A lot of people knew by this time. I actually went out of my way to get their gifts professionally wrapped.

The Christmas meal was set out on red and gold tableware. Back then, our tradition was that before we ate, somebody at the table would start the prayer and everybody around the table would put in a word to continue the prayer. Of course, I followed. Then dessert time was when we opened up gifts. So, I handed out my gifts to everyone. I handed it out to the kids first. I just got them toys, books and some clothes.

Most of the adults, my cousins and others, got perfumes or colognes or something to go with their electronics or a gift card. My aunt and my grandmother received the same gift. It was the Elizabeth Taylor white diamonds perfume 100ml and a cashmere shawl. Now as I said, I had something planned for my grandmother. For her gift, I left the security alarm on the shawl and the price tag of $382. Even though my aunt and her received the same style shawl, hers was blue, purple and yellow, with a touch of white.

My aunt's was pink, gray and white. My aunt opened hers and she put on her shawl and she thanked me. She liked the color and she loved the perfume. My grandmother now began to open up her shawl. While opening it, she saw the alarm tag. She said, "Well, mine has this on it! How am I going to take this off?"

And I said to her, "Oh, that's okay. Pass it to me." Me being the booster that I am, the alarm tags were not really a challenge. I could take them off with my hands. So I took the shawl from her and I folded one end and then I opened the other end where the security tag was and pulled it really hard. In two to three clicks, it was off the garment. Right as I stood in front of her, I removed the piece with the pin and I took off the other piece.

I put it back together and I said, "You know, I don't want anything to happen up in there so I will take it with me and throw it away later." My grandmother was pleased and she was happy and she even wanted to take a photo with the cashmere shawl. Everybody took a picture, a group picture, and I stood beside her while the picture was taken to show Helen, my godmother, who usually comes to Christmas dinner, but she couldn't make it that year. She had left the country to go to the US.

After the picture, they began to finish off the desserts and those that were having seconds went back for more. I strategically waited a half an hour and then I said, "I'm going to be going soon." I didn't get a lot of gifts from them. I received a card from my aunt and a card from my cousin. In the card was just a visa gift card that had "Merry Christmas'' written on it. My aunt then asked me if I wanted to take food home. Of course, I said, "Pack up the things that I like."

I then turned to my grandmother, "I find it so strange. Last Christmas, you crucified not only me, but my mother, my father and my siblings for being like my mother. You claim to be a woman of God and you further say that you guys are holy and sanctified. But yet you sat here and watched me take off a security tag off an expensive item. In fact, I saw you glimpse at the tag to see how much it was - truth be told, I left it there on purpose to see what you would do. You watched me disable it, then threw it back around your shoulder, took many photos - even a photo of me and you standing up. But yet, you're a holy, sanctified, miss evangelist."

Immediately, I could see the sweat building up on her nose. She was angry. I said, "The truth hurts, but it also looks good doesn't it? You're no better than your daughter and no better than me, miss church choir and youth leader. You should have never accepted my gifts. Period. Much less accept a gift that had a security tag on it, watch me disable it, and still take photos. Now, how would Mister James feel about this?"

She got angry and she said, "Oh I don't want those photos to be printed." At that time, you still had to print the photos. She said she was going to burn the cashmere.

"So if I said nothing, you would have packed up the leftovers and left with a cashmere shawl on your neck, but because I exposed you, the person you really are, now it's a problem?" I turned to everybody and I said "Good evening ladies, gentlemen and well-wishers. This will be my last Christmas dinner with you bag of fucking hypocrites. I don't want your leftovers and I don't want anything to do with anybody in this room."

I picked up my keys and I laughed all the way to the door. My aunt was trying to stop me on the way to the door. They wanted me to explain and they wanted to get my grandmother to apologize. My grandmother was still riled up. When I got to the door, my aunt came outside chuckling. "You know what, Kamelah? This is really something your mother would have done." I could hear my grandmother inside because the door wasn't closed all the way. I actually heard her curse at me so I peeked back through the door just a little bit. Just so she could see my nose and one of my eyes.

I peeked and said "There you go. There's the real you! Come on! If you want a problem you can come outside! Good God of Daniel, the real you has arrived!"

.I could honestly say I wasn't paying attention to what my aunt was saying. I really wanted to hear what lies she was telling her friends from work as well as friends from our community who were also at this big Christmas dinner. There were over 50 people at my aunt's home. So everybody was in an uproar while she was trying to explain herself but not everybody was in the room. Some were downstairs, so not everybody knew the full extent of me taking off the security tag but, people started asking questions and you know me being the black sheep of the family, people started asking, "What did Kamelah do?" Those that heard our confrontation tried to explain. I could hear them all bickering and overheard my grandmother curse again.

I said, "The blood of Jesus is against you. The devil is a liar, and so is his mother."

While I was laughing, I had stopped listening. I didn't care any longer to be honest. I turned to my aunt and I said, "Did your mother tell you? This spring and summer I stopped by her house and I gifted her with shower curtains, a bathroom set, bathroom mats, kitchen mats, and even a pot set."

She said, "Not really."

I said, "Yeah, so go inside. Not all the way and ask her. Did she give you these things?"

She said, "No, I'm not gonna do that. I will ask her later."

I said, "No, I would like you to do it. That's the one request I have for you. I don't ask for much from you guys at all. I don't even ask for you guys to pray for me. Because not every prayer is a good prayer. Clearly the devil is in there, I don't even want you to crack the door. I want you to go inside, face the devil, and ask her about my visits this spring and summer. She opened the house door slowly, "Did Kamelah visit you and give a bathroom curtain? Then she asked if I even helped her put it up.

I yelled from outside, "She never once asked for a receipt! Never once asked where I got it from but asked if I could get more for her barrel to send back home! Yet last Christmas, she sat here, and she put me, my mother, my siblings, and my father's name in the dirt. Behind your guys' backs, she is the devil! She only acts like she's holy in front of you guys!"

She had no answer to her daughter asking her about her ungodly acts. My aunt looked back at me and said, "Promise me that if I leave you out here for a minute you won't leave" I respected my aunt. I did. But a promise is a comfort to a fool and I was about done with the foolery that was going on. That was it, I never returned to that door ever again. I never returned to a Christmas or Thanksgiving, not even an Easter brunch. I was invited but declined each time. Some of my family members would see me in the community because my grandmother still lived in the Jane and Finch area. But, I had nothing to say and by the look of my face, they would not dare to try me.

CHAPTER 8:

STICKS AND STONES

My godmother had a friend named Mrs. Liz out in Newmarket who lived about 14 houses down from us. She would order stuff from me for her children, for her grandchildren and even for herself behind my godmother's back. I never told my godmother because she was one of my monthly customers in my $500 book - meaning her order was usually $500 or more. My godmother was out in Vancouver for 3 weeks and so I decided to pass by just to check up on the house. I saw that the leaves needed to be cleaned up. So I went to the garage, and I looked for the paper bags. In certain parts of the city, you have to put out leaves in certain paper bags. Well in the hood, we didn't care about that at all. I looked for the paper bags and I couldn't find them. So I just said to myself, "You know what? I'll just pack them up in the garbage bags and bring them down to Toronto with me to throw them out."

While doing that, the lady across from me, Mrs. Saraino, a very fragile, small Italian lady said hi to me. Sometimes when she'd see me, she'd call me different names. But, I'd still answer her because I really liked her. While I was cleaning up the leaves in garbage bags and placing them close to the car, Mrs. Saraino greeted me again saying, "Hi!" She was now louder than before. She clearly wanted my attention. She said, "Kristine!!"

I replied, "Hi, how are you Mrs. Saraino?"

"I'm doing well." "You're cleaning up the lawn?"

I said, "Yeah, something like that. I saw a few leaves on her lawn and driveway. You want me to do yours?"

She said, "Oh, that would be amazing. That would be awesome."

Her son was out of the house for over a year; he would usually be the one to do it for her. While I was cleaning up, she was telling me old stories from the 60's and something else that I had probably heard 1000 times. Still, I gave her the attention that she needed. I ended up with half a garbage bag of leaves from her and I packed them up as well. She offered me some water. We drank and she continued to talk. This was all in under 20 minutes or less. We said our goodbyes and I then crossed the street to finish cleaning my grandmother's lawn.

One of the garbage bags was actually garbage that was in the garage. While I was getting ready to pack the bags in the back of my car, Mrs. Liz passed by with her fancy car and she greeted me with just a wave and I smiled and waved back and she went about her way. That evening, I received a phone call from my godmother. Of course I answered just in case she was checking in. It turned out that she was really upset. I said "What happened now?"

She said to me, "You know I don't agree with those things and I told you don't bring those things to the house."

"What are you talking about?" I'm totally confused.

"Mrs. Liz told me that she passed by today and you had all your goods in garbage bags at the front of the door."

"Oh, Really? That never happened and I'm not going to have this conversation with you now because you're upset. I'll see you when you get back."

She went on but I did not hear one word until she called my name. 2 weeks later when she landed she called me to let me know she got home safe and to come see her. I went for the next three days. When I went up there, she was no longer upset. My godmother does not carry too much anger. I asked her how her day was. Before she could answer, I asked "What did Liz say I did now?"

She was like, "Oh, just forget about it."

I replied, "Oh no, I don't want to forget about it because you called me angry. First and foremost, it's a bold faced lie." I said, "I want you to tell me again in detail what she said I did or what she said she saw." My godmother said, "Kamelah, I really don't want to speak about it."

I expressed myself in a calm manner, "I understand you don't want to speak about it. I understand it's your friend. However, the situation that your friend presented to you is something that I thought you knew I would never do."

And so she said, "This is why I want to talk about it. I was angry in the moment. I wanted to apologize for it." I let her know, "I respect that you want to apologize but I would still like to know what your church sister said to you."

She then told me, "I can see that you are not going to let this go." Nope! She continued, "Liz said she was coming up the road and she saw you and so she stopped and she greeted you. You guys had a small chat. And you were picking up bags out of your car and bringing it to the house and putting them close to the lawn because they were heavy and you look startled to see her. That's all."

"Oh. Okay" I said, "So where did 'stolen goods' come in?""

"Because Liz said, "The only thing that could be in that big bag that would be so heavy was stolen goods."

I explained, "This is a big joke, but I'm glad that she was concerned - actually pleased. Now put on your house slippers. Let's go across the street."

She was questioning me, "What are we going across the street for?" "Because I would like to present to you what really happened that day."

Of course, she was confused and hesitant at first but she put on her brown house slippers. And so, we went across to the street to see Mrs. Saraino. Of course we spoke first, and again, she had a story from the 60's to the 50's. I cut the stories after 5 minutes. "Mrs. Saraino, do you remember when I was here a few weeks ago, and I helped with the lawn?" She paused and said, "Oh, yes!" She stood up and said to my godmother, "You have the most amazing daughter. You know, she helped me and my son didn't even help me clean up. He's a lazy brute. She cleaned up the lawn. It wasn't a lot of leaves, but she had so many from your lawn. You know, you should look into getting a landscaper. She put them in the garbage bags. You should teach her that they go in the big paper bags. She asked me if I had garbage bags and I told her, "No, it wasn't that much. I mostly had compost bags; more than the garbage bags that I used for my garden." Then, she went on to talk about her garden.

I saw my godmother's face. She put down her head and shook it. Of course, I laughed, excused myself, and walked away. Mrs. Sanrino said, "It was a good day, wasn't it?!"

I replied, "Yes, it was. It was a good day indeed. Today is an even better day for me."

I left them over there talking and I came over to the house. I sat in the kitchen and I waited five or ten minutes. My godmother came in. She said, "I know I apologized to you earlier, but I want to apologize again."

I said, "No, it's okay. You know, regardless of what people think of me, if she saw me doing something wrong as an adult, she should have scolded me rather than calling you while you were on vacation at that. But that's fine."

My godmother said, "Don't say anything to her." I smiled "Me?! I would never say anything to her."

I was livid - beyond mad! But I didn't want my godmother to see that. I actually spent the night there. In the morning, we had breakfast and I left in the afternoon. Almost a year had passed and Easter was coming. Liz owed me $200 that she failed to report to my godmother along with the goods, the stolen goods, I had brought to her home with her well-manicured lawn out front.

That Easter, I told my godmother, "I'm coming to church with you, I will meet you at church." She said, "You sure? Because you always say you're coming…" I said, "I'm coming, you can count on me. I will be there."

While I was driving to church, I thought of all the things that I'd given to Liz. Her daughter was strung out on drugs and I never judged her because I knew that my friend had passed away from drugs. She had custody of her 5 grandchildren. When Liz came to me and asked me for assistance for the children, I was incomplete shock. Even though I had a set price, when it came to Liz, I dealt with her really nicely. If six outfits were priced for $100, I would give Liz 9 outfits for that price. All her church dresses were coming from high end stores.

I got to the church a little bit late on purpose that day. Praise and worship was an hour long and Mrs. Liz was in the choir. I wore jeans and a nice blouse with flowers on it. I was never one to do my hair but that morning, I spent a little bit of time on my hair and I made sure I had on lip gloss because I wanted everybody to be able to read my lips in case they could not hear me.

I walked into church - straight to the altar. That altar was pretty high. Considering the fact that I'm 5'5", with me standing, it was surprising that the altar was at chest level. I walked in and I didn't know if my godmother saw me. By the time I got to the altar, she probably thought I was going in for a word of prayer because I raised my hand as they were singing and I was singing too. Then when the pastor came my way to rest his hand on my head, I held his hand and I said, "I have a testimony. Glory be to God I am pleased!" He stopped the music.

He said to the congregation, "Look, this young lady has a testimony! We have not seen you in a long time, my child. What is the testimony you want to give to me on this glorious morning?"

I said, "You know what, Pastor? I've also been praying." I glanced up and I saw Liz with her fan. Her eyes were wide open and she had my stolen goods on. Because it was Easter, she had on a purple and yellow dress that I had got her. I knew the price was $479.99 and I knew what store I got it from.

He said, "We've been praying for you too." Because I speak fast, I chose to say my words slowly. What could have been a minute, probably became five. I said, "Yes, the law says that I am a klepto, and I pray sometimes that the spirit of me being a klepto will go away. And that I will no longer steal."

The pastor shouted "My God!" I said, "Well..." and I paused very dramatically...

I said, "Well, sister Liz helped me out. I'm grateful for her kindness monthly." I could feel my godmother coming down the aisles- "She owes me $200 for the dress that she's wearing up there with my stolen goods. Look at her tag! It's from Candies Bridal. She has been getting goods from me for her grandchildren and her children for over 2 years and demanded that I lie to my mother, but because Liz paid me so well, it's so hard for me to stop stealing."

I could hear it clear as day, my godmother in the background "Kamelah!!!!" I could hear her footsteps now - it sounded like she was running down the aisle. I did not care. I could hear the gasps and whispering from the congregation. They were trying to grab the mic but I kept on talking.

I pulled out my cell phone and I said, "She texted me her new order 4 days ago. She saw me the other day, packing up leaves on my mother's lawn, and she decided to take false news to my godmother for my godmother to scold me. I still want the $200 that I worked for."

My godmother was tugging at me and I was still walking midway down the aisle now and I didn't give two rats' eyelashes. My godmother was saying to me, "This is embarrassing! Why would you do this?"

We were now in the church lobby and all the sisters were going on like: "What is this?" "What's going on?" "I'm going to look at her tag!" "Watch you!" "You're ready to convict her though!" I thought to myself, look at you guys. They didn't say much to me because a few of them were also good customers from time to time.

My godmother said to me, "If this is over $200, I'll give it to you. I'll even give you $300…"

I cut her off and I said, "No, I don't want no money. I would really appreciate when you all are talking about me that you remember this" I said, as I pointed to the crowd in the hall. "When Jesus died on the cross, there was a thief and a murderer beside him. Let he who is without sin please cast the first stone. I am at peace. It is well."

I never felt like I was welcome back at that church and I never returned there anyway. I never spoke to Ms. Liz again. She and my godmother had a falling out because of the situation. I didn't see my godmother anymore. I didn't even return her calls until Christmas. Even when she had questions I would say, "If you want answers to your questions, I can give you my phone and you can read every order your church sister ordered from me and you can question your friend. She should have never told you that bold-faced lie because I would never put you in harm's way or bring things to your home."

If I ever gave my godmother something, the first thing she'd ask me is, "Where's the receipt for this?" I had to present the receipt so often that I started to put it in the envelope as part of the gift. "Here's the gift, and here's the receipt too!" I would say jokingly. Liz's husband offered me my $200 back. He came to my godmother's house one time when I was there after the scene at the church.

He said, "Hello Kamelah, how are you?" I never had anything against him. But while he was offering me the money, I looked up at him, and noticed he had on a shirt that I happened to be very familiar with., But, I wasn't about to say to his face, "You have stolen goods on."

I just told him, "No, it's okay. I'm over it. It's in the past, let it be." As I said:

"Let he who is without sin cast the first stone" - John 8:7

CHAPTER 9:

A COUPLE OF COUPLES

It was prom time, not for me, but for a friend of mine. She was much older than me - Cynthia - and she was going with her man, Dwayne. They were high school sweethearts. Their prom was actually their wedding and I got invited. Cynthia was about 5'3" and soft spoken with a nice cool chocolate complexion that was flawless. She was highly intelligent and actually skipped 3 grades to graduate early.

After high school, she studied to become a nurse and went on to start her own practice. Dwayne's family was well off, his family owned a very popular food chain. He was also smart. He was an engineer so he could fix lots of things like cars, electronics, etc. He was good with his hands. Cynthia and Dwayne were financially stable as both had careers and came from good families They moved far out of town to a ranch-style home with acres of land. They went on to have a family and her last daughter was my godchild.

Throughout the relationship, she would complain a lot about his infidelity and his cheating ways. He ended up having a son in Atlanta and Cynthia just accepted him as her own son. Cynthia was also close to a couple of my family members as we were from the same community growing up. We grew up in the suburbs and so we would check up on each other from time to time. I didn't really visit the ranch that often because it was a far drive, but it was beautiful. It had 6 bedrooms and each room had its own bathroom. The ranch had 2 kitchens and a pool. Her wedding picture was 5 ft. x 6 ft. and it was hanging in the big foyer with a staircase on each side.

She spoke intelligently, but she was the hood – just the bougie kind of hood. Her background was Jamaican but it only came out when she got together with a few of us.

She would occasionally call to check in on me, to tell me about the kids and her travels, and to ask what was going on, how so and so was, to ask about events or just to complain about Dwayne.

This particular summer, she said she was going on a cruise with her husband in an effort to work things out. When she returned, I received a phone call from her... at 3 o'clock in the morning. She was crying and I asked her, "Cynthia, what's wrong?" She was so upset that her words were not coming out of her mouth; they barely escaped one word at a time.

I heard her say the name Dwayne and I heard her mumble "I can't believe this." She asked me to come out there at 3 o'clock in the morning to see her. I thought to myself, there's no way I'm driving out there at this hour. They don't even have lights out there in the boonies where they lived.

So I asked her again, "What's wrong?" Cynthia couldn't speak clearly, but I could tell that something was really off. Cynthia and I had a mutual friend named Wendy, so I told Cynthia, "I'm going to try and call her, although it's late and I'm not sure she'll be up." After a couple attempts, she did answer the phone. "What did you do for you to be calling me this late? How much is your bail?"

I said to her, "Even in your sleep you got jokes… it's not me it's Cynthia. She's not even speaking a full sentence; it's like she left her voice on vacation. Who has jokes now? Haha, sorry my bad. I don't know what's going on, but she's crying hysterically. Let me connect the call, she's on the other line."

We could hear Dwayne, although faint, in the background. Wendy asked her if she was ok and what had transpired but it was the same answer from Cynthia, "I can't believe this."

I told Wendy, "Cynthia was asking for me to come up there, but you love to drive. Can you go up there? I'll come up in the morning around 6am."

Wendy said, "Of course, no problem." And then she set off to the ranch. I stayed on the phone until Wendy got to Cynthia's. She still wasn't able to complete a full sentence so I still had no idea what was going on. The phone number I had for Dwayne was out of service.

Cynthia said to me, "I'll call you back." I asked, "Are you sure? I don't feel comfortable with you coming off of the phone. Is everything okay?"

She said to me, "Everything is not okay, but I do have to call you back, just give me 2 minutes." So I began to pick out some clothes and called Wendy to see how far she was. It was now 4:30 am. I hadn't heard from Wendy, so I called her "Hello - Wendy what are you eating?!"

With her mouth full she uttered, "a 12-grain bagel…"

I cut her off and asked, "How far are you from the ranch?"

"I'm 15 minutes away from Cynthia's place," she said. "Did she tell you what's wrong?"

I answered, "She's not even speaking English. I just don't want to drive in the dark and the sun is going to come up soon. So, I'm going to take a shower and get ready." Then the phone beeped, so I three-wayed the phone call. Cynthia was still crying.

Now Wendy was asking, "What am I about to walk into? I'm like 10 minutes away and I have coffee, bagels, and a few muffins…."

Wendy shut up when Cynthia asked, "You're 10 minutes away?" That's the only full sentence she could muster up since she first called.

Wendy went on to ask her "Cynthia are you hurt?"

"No."

"Is there a crime scene?" Also no.

"Wendy, it's a bit late for you to be 10 minutes away with a car full of food!"

Well, I certainly didn't want to be there if there's a crime scene in that neighborhood, I thought to myself. "Go get ready." Wendy said. "I'm going to talk to her and when I get some information, I'll call you while you're on your way up."

I finally started to feel some relief because I knew somebody was there with Cynthia. Wendy called probably an hour after she arrived at the ranch. Right then, it was almost 5:30 in the morning. I was already on my way and obviously I put on a track suit and sneakers. I was 20 minutes away. "What happened?!" I asked.

"Well, there's a situation with Dwayne and Cynthia. I can't control it. We need to be here."

Wendy was a very posh 5'7" and a complete beauty. She was an amazing listener with good advice. She didn't curse and had a kind heart and always had her hair in a bun. I was now beginning to hear Dwayne over the phone, but I also heard another voice besides Dwayne's. It sounded vaguely like his friend Trevor. Trevor was the best man at Cynthia and Dwayne's wedding. He was somebody that I didn't see too often, but he lived much closer to them than we did. He didn't come back to the hood. Even though we went to the same after school program, this would be my first time seeing him since the wedding. Trevor was the godfather for all of the children too, even Dwayne's child out of wedlock.

I heard Trevor in the background yelling at the top of his voice which got me riled up. "Wendy, who is he yelling at? Excuse me?!" That made me press on the gas. I was supposed to be doing 50 mph, but I started pushing 80 mph. There was just so much confusion and all I could hear was Cynthia crying, Wendy saying 'ok calm down', and the voices of the kids also started coming through... It was a lonely 2-way road. I noticed at one point that I was doing 100 mph. I finally got there to the ranch about 15 minutes later and heard a lot of screaming and yelling and crying - from Cynthia. My initial thought was, "Did Cynthia drink a gallon of water? She'd been bawling her eyes out since 3 am. What's the problem?"

Wendy pulled me aside. While doing so, Trevor approached me, "You ghetto rat. What are you doing up here? What are they calling you for? Did you bring your gangsters with you?"

I turned to him and said, "I'll deal with you later. Wendy, what's going on?" Mind you, as loud as we're getting, there were no neighbors around to hear. I asked, "Are the kids going to school?" It was almost 8 o'clock in the morning. "Okay, what are we doing? There were a lot of adults arguing and there were kids in the house.

Some of the bigger kids had to go to school, the smaller ones didn't, Wendy was like, "I don't know, does a school bus come out this far?" I sorted that out really quick. I didn't know what to make for lunch so I just gave them $10 each and wished them a good day at school.

The kids were set so I revisited the question, "What's going on now?" Wendy was still trying to keep everybody apart. I mean, people were shoving people and people were yelling and Cynthia was just sitting down rocking and crying. There was only one child in the house but at the time, she was almost one years old with the nanny upstairs.

The tension in the room was at an all-time high and I could feel my heart racing. Wendy took my hand and said to me, "Kamelah, she handed this to me as I got in the door. I would rather show you. I was waiting for you to watch it." Trevor was still hysterical and I really had to block out all the noise. Wendy took me to the other room. This was a big house so their yelling soon became whispers. Trevor was trying to get to Wendy, she had this DVD in her hand that he was trying to grab from her.

I finally put my foot down, "Let me tell you guys something. I don't care about any of the back and forth yelling and lame attempts to fight. Put in the damn DVD and let's get this over with."

Cynthia stood up and spoke, "It was the best thing I ever invested in. The truth always sets you free." Finally, I thought, but that's all you had to say after 6 hours? Maybe I shouldn't have yelled at her but the whole situation was just too much for me.

I couldn't deal with everyone just yelling. "Wendy, just push the damn DVD in already."

Once the DVD went in, Cynthia's crying then became weeping and moaning. I braced myself, 'Okay, what am I about to see?' I looked at the 70-inch TV mounted to the wall.

Cynthia jumped in front of the screen, paused the video and said, "No wait. Can you tell the nanny to take the baby to the park or on a walk please? I don't want that to play while she's here. "

I went to the nanny. "We're having a discussion amongst adults, is it possible…"

And before I could finish, she said, "No problem, is everything okay?"

I said, "Of course, everything is fine." So, the nanny got the baby dressed and packed a bag with toys and snacks and took the baby to the park.

When she finally left, I took off my hoodie, turned off my other cell phone, looked at the adults and said, "Let me tell you guys something. if you don't press play, I'm leaving because this is taking way too long. I've been here for hours and I'm hot."

Cynthia cleared her throat, "You don't have to press play, I'm going to tell you. I have a hidden camera in the house. I actually had it for the nanny. But um, it caught some stuff on camera…" She was speaking so eloquently like it was an acceptance speech. She said, "I'm just so disappointed in Dwayne's actions. I should have known better. I wonder if I drove him to this."

I said to her, "I drove up here. Wendy drove up here. Could we see what the problem is?" I'd finally calmed down because Cynthia was no longer hysterical and she was speaking complete sentences. She had this calmness about her and so I knew I didn't need to be rowdy anymore.

She said, "Well, press play, you can see for yourself." Wendy got another muffin and took a deep sigh and a bite.

The security camera footage showed Dwayne and Trevor playing gracefully in lingerie. Then they started kissing while lying in the living room . For the first time in my life, my jaw literally dropped, I was speechless. Wendy began screaming and she paused the video there and yelled, "OH HELL NO! You've gotta be fucking kidding me!"

I applauded her, "Wendy, you can curse!! What?!" But then I sat down slowly.

Cynthia had black leather couches in her house, but they were La-Z-Boy couches, so when you sat back too far, the feet would flip up. I didn't even notice that the feet of the chair popped up, I just took a moment of silence to truly digest what I had seen.... Then hood Kamelah snapped back into her role as Trevor became upset all over again yelling and cursing back and forth downstairs. I turned to Cynthia, "Why are you thinking this is your fault?!" She started crying again. So I said, "You go on and be sad, you have a right to cry," I said while getting up to hug her.

Trevor then stormed back into the room where we were sitting shouting, "So what? You're no good anyway! He never wanted you! He's never going to want you!" Trevor was trying to get to Cynthia and Cynthia was just sitting there not even defending herself. But he had to try to go through me and Wendy to get to her. There was a letter opener on the desk closest to Cynthia and she picked it up because Trevor was just doing the most. He was all over the place, hopping, skipping, jumping and cursing.

He was yelling and so was Dwayne saying, "You drove me to do this!"

I started yelling and again, no one was even hearing each other anymore. I was ready to fight, but no one wanted to fight me. Trevor hit Cynthia so she swung back and ended up cutting Trevor's hand with the letter opener. I kicked him so swift he fell before I could kick him again. Wendy pulled me back. "I'm calling the police!" Trevor said, and he did!

When the police came, they took him and his paper cut outside, while Wendy, Cynthia and I stayed inside. The police officers ended up coming inside. In my head I was thinking, Another crime scene… Why do I always seem to end up at these? Do I give these guys my real name, because if they type me up…Oh my Jesus. They came to talk to us just to get our side of the story. I told them up front, ``I just came up here to make sure my friend was safe." I for sure didn't give them my real name.

Wendy explained what we witnessed. I said, "It's basically self-defense. He was attacking her, and he's a male. She didn't even intentionally point the letter opener at him. She just had it in her hand because he kept flashing his hands close to her face, you can see it's not a big cut."

The police said, "We just want to know what's going on here. Is this domestic or are they brothers…?"

I said, "No, they're lovers."

The police officers turned red immediately. One said, "Excuse me?" Wendy explained what had just been revealed and everyone went into their feelings and absolute shock.

The police officer said, "Well, he wants to charge her for assault. I have to look into it because he does have a cut. We called the medic to check him out."

I chimed in, "Are you really going to arrest her on her own property, in her own home, after what she just told you?!"

He said, "I have somebody outside." I didn't even realize the ambulance had come. There was an ambulance and a fire truck. The officer said, "I have somebody outside who's saying that somebody assaulted them and there is physical evidence of them being assaulted." You've got to be kidding me...I thought. Meanwhile, I'm waiting for Trevor to say I kicked him - I already had my lawyer's number pulled up on my phone.

He said to Cynthia, "I won't handcuff you, but I do have to place you under arrest. It's just the law." I was in complete disarray. Like what?! The officer went on to say that Trevor and Dwayne said the attack was because they were gay and wanted to leave and that it amounted to a hate crime. I was just trying to remain calm; we didn't know this about him until 30 minutes ago. A hate crime?! Calm down…

CHAPTER 10:

BROKEN GLASS

They found out quickly that Cynthia didn't have a criminal record... She didn't even have a driving record. She was at the station for a couple of hours. The nanny would be able to handle the children "What are we gonna do?" I asked.

Wendy suggested that we destroy the tape. "You watch way too much TV," I explained. "We can't destroy the tape. It's evidence."

"Okay, well don't play the tape, I don't want to see it anymore." So, I returned to my nurturing mode. I opened the double door fridge that was embedded in the closet. The nanny was back. She also helped me in the kitchen make BBQ chicken and macaroni pie for the kids before they came home. "We need to tell Cynthia's mother," I suggested to Wendy, "because what if they hold her for a while and she needs bail?" God knows I couldn't help her with that.

The nanny handed me the phone - it was Cynthia. She was back to not speaking in full sentences. I put the phone on speaker and the officer came on the phone.

"This is officer Lindale; I think your friend is in a state of shock. We can't get any answers from her. But we have the complainants, Trevor and Dwayne…" What was Dwayne doing there with him? This was the mother of his children. The officer continued, "They both want to press charges, so she'll have court in the morning." I was so disappointed in the law.

The officer went on to say "Since she's not responsive, we have to hold her for a psych evaluation. We don't think she's safe to be with herself or anybody else." Look who's not going home again today, I thought to myself as I called my lawyer for her.

This ended up being a 4-day process. Wendy and I drove back and forth to court in her car. I had my kids and school to deal with and I saw that Frank had called me a few times but this was bigger than all that I had going on. That Friday, Cynthia was released on her own accord. I told Wendy to take her home, "I'm going to get my kids and stay here for the weekend. The kids can play with their kids, ride horses and enjoy the fresh air."

Late that night, we were woken up by the sound of glass shattering. I'm thinking someone was trying to break into the house. We looked over the banister to see Cynthia standing in front of her wedding photo. She had smashed it. She was finally speaking - the language of fury.

I then noticed that she was with her middle daughter and she asked her, "Can you share with them why you think I'm mad?" Wendy and I looked at each other because she had returned to speaking full sentences. "Oh, where are my manners? Good morning ladies, how are you?" She said to her daughter again, "You can tell your aunts why you think I'm mad at your dad." She said it very calmly, like nothing had been going on and like she didn't just smash up a 6-foot tall photo.

Cynthia and her daughter were sitting on the plush living room carpet and we sat on the couch to be closer to them. So, I asked the daughter, "Tell me why you think your mom is mad at your dad or why your dad's mad at your mom?"

She said, "I think it's because when Uncle Trevor bought us our bicycles and helped us put it together that day, we came back from the park from skipping ropes and chalk and we saw them playing in mommy's panties. They said that they bought it for a gift and that they were trying it on first." Uncle Trevor gave us $50 each and said, "Don't tell mommy, we would ruin the surprise." Wendy started to cry. I told the child she could go upstairs and get ready to eat breakfast.

While walking away she asked, "So mommy wasn't surprised about the gift anymore because I saw it already?" Cynthia let out a sharp scream that ripped through my body.

Wendy then asked, "Is that the only time that you've seen them playing with your mommy's gifts?" She said, "No, Uncle Trevor always came over, and he and daddy wrestled in the basement." I was so angry. Wendy continued questioning, and I just went blank. I drifted in thought back to the situation I was once in, in that closet locked up by Jermaine. The emotions took me right back to that moment and I forgot where I was.

When I came back, Wendy was on the phone crying and Cynthia wasn't even responding. She was just shaking. Wendy was trying to console Cynthia. I don't know how long I blacked out, but Cynthia looked at me and asked, "Kamelah, are you okay?"

I said, "Am I okay? I'm fine…." she interrupted,

"But you're crying, I never see you cry."

"I don't know what you're talking about. As long as you're ok, I will be fine" and I wiped my tears away.

Cynthia said, "I want to rest." She had a throw blanket on the other end of the sofa, she was pointing to it and she laid there until she fell asleep. Wendy was just walking around in circles because she didn't know what to do and I was sitting on the carpet looking out into space. What Cynthia's daughter said just kept on replaying over and over and each time it got louder and louder in my head. I felt myself getting angry. I thought so hard that I blacked out again.

The next thing I remembered, Wendy was tapping my foot saying to me, "The phone, the phone…Cynthia's mom wants to speak to you." I tried to piece my thoughts back together. Wendy didn't understand a lick of Jamaican, so she didn't understand what Mrs. Thompson was saying. Mrs. Thompson was very much upset, the number of curse words coming out of her mouth were uncountable, "And this boxsie gal just a bawl all me a talk to har she nah answer, a weh dis fada god." She asked that we look into getting a flight to come up ASAP. Wendy was already at the computer.

The week finally passed. I ended up driving Wendy's car back to the city to drop off my children and then returned right back to Cynthia's. In that three to four days' time, Cynthia had a visitor, who was one of her doctor colleagues. He turned to us and said, "I don't know what happened before, but she's definitely in a state of shock, and if she doesn't get help, it's not gonna get any better."

She had also received a letter that Dwayne had filed for divorce. Of course, both gentlemen came to court, and by this time, Cynthia's mom came from Jamaica to help out with the children and console her daughter. I tried my best to go there as much as possible and so did Wendy. In divorce court, they fought over everything, down to the landscaper. He blamed Cynthia for him turning to Trevor - because she's boring - and she didn't have time for him. Cynthia's mom had a few real Jamacian Kingstonian outbursts in that courtroom where we had to go on recess a few times because she was cussing and angry, but no one could understand her. At one point, the judge asked if there was a translator. When they asked me to translate, I said that "I'd rather not say." She was upset that her daughter was not confined to a mental hospital.

What I thought to be nice was that Dwayne's baby mother from Atlanta had come for support. She expressed that he was bisexual and that he had told her. When she told him she was pregnant, he begged her to have an abortion - hence why they didn't have the best relationship. But, she made it very clear to the court that he never hid his sexuality while in Atlanta.

Cynthia spoke twice at court. Once when she was asked if she wished to tell the truth and again when she said, "I wish to give him nothing that I worked for." Everything else was answered by her nurse. Throughout that year, she didn't speak. When visiting her, we would bring her a few books to read, plus puzzles and fashion magazines.

This dear friend of mine that was about 180 pounds was now on average 90 pounds. Her hair was full of salt and pepper gray. And, she refused to let her children visit her, not wanting them to see her like that. I made it a point of duty on her birthday to visit her and I always visited her a day before my birthday. I did get angry with her on a few occasions saying, "I need you to snap outta this. I need you to be the mother that I know, and I need you to be the friend that I adore. I don't like to see you like this." While speaking to her, I could just look at her eyes and feel her pain. Sometimes she smiled, and sometimes she cried. I knew that crying was a language. I didn't know what language she was speaking at that moment. The hate crime and assault charges were dropped.

Years passed and Cynthia's mom would call me at least two times a week. She would rather speak in person just for company's sake. One time, when visiting Cynthia with Wendy, Wendy who had gotten there before me said, "She forgot that you were coming today. But, she said thanks." "Wow, she talked to you?" I asked.

"There wasn't a lot of talking, she just said, 'I owe you guys gas money for coming up here that morning. Thanks you guys.'"

I could see from the room that she was smiling, so I knew that she knew that Wendy had already passed along her message. I just shook my head and said, "Look at the things that you're worried about! Gas money?" We all smiled. I played some music from my phone and we did silly things. Either dancing or telling jokes, or filling her in on what was going on in the hood. She always liked my hood stories. They were amazing to her because she was so posh. Wendy and I just sat there looking at Cynthia for about half an hour. She basically smiled until she fell asleep.

I've only ever seen Trevor once. I'd seen Dwayne a few times. The first time I saw him after their court date, I was very vocal of course. From a distance, I was very careful with things that I said because I knew what those two were capable of.

Another time at the airport, I saw he was with another individual other than Trevor. When I saw Trevor, he had something to say, but I refused to answer him. "Cynthia is still not well. I still keep her in my prayers." I said nothing but slowly gave him the middle finger. Cynthia's mother became her power of attorney and she sold her ranch with all of her things - it was at Cynthia's request that none of the furniture be moved into a new home. Years later, she was still in the mental health clinic. She was basically doing a life sentence for a broken heart. I didn't know when she would get bail for herself. All I could be was a friend with a phone call or a visit.

CHAPTER 11:

BLACKOUTS

My dreams became so real that I would wake up and it would be my grandmother just having a full conversation with me telling me things I shouldn't do or people I shouldn't speak to. My grandmother always told me, even when she was alive, to try to limit my cursing from my mouth. Not everything that comes to your mind you have to say out loud!" Even in spirit, she would still remind me, "Tiny, do you have to curse this much? You know, not every fight you have to show up for." I never met my grandfather but he would occasionally talk with my uncle just saying how proud they were and what not to do.

During this time of blacking out, I would find myself back in the same space of being in the presence of Jermaine with his and my friends' mom in the same room. But now, I was alone in the room and my uncle was saying, "Tiny, run!" This just kept happening over and over. Early one morning, I had a vision of my uncle pushing Jermaine to apologize for his actions. Jermaine was being hesitant, even beyond the grave, this man was still a damn nuisance.

Jermaine wore the same outfit and spoke to me saying, "She should have stayed home, I don't have to apologize." A knock at my door stopped the vision.

"It's FedEx with registered mail for Kamelah."

I answered, "I don't need to open it, I know who it's from." I really needed to turn on that phone at some point - just not right now.

While sleep became an enemy, I still had to try to fight through it. I told my pastor and godmother to pray for me. In the morning, my grandmother said to me," I'm tired."

"Momma, Why are you tired? Why mamma?" I asked.

"I have to walk behind you so much. Sometimes, I have to walk in front of you. Can you slow down Tiny, so I can just take a break? I'm tired."

"A break from what?" I asked. She never answered. I felt bad and weird at the same time.

That same week, I went to the mall. I had on a jean skirt, it had stripes and stars on it. Something like the American flag. I also had on a white spaghetti strapped top. I had $2,000 of orders to do for a few people. This lady came up to me and said, "What does that mean on your neck?"

"Well, good afternoon to you too." I replied.

"Sorry, good afternoon, how's your day thus far?"

"My day's just beginning, how's your day going?" I asked her.

"It's great. What does that mean on your neck?"

On my neck, I had a tattoo of Psalm 41:1. I said to her like I said to everybody, "Well, it's your homework."

She smiled and asked, "Okay, so what's that on your arm?"

"Miss, I'm about to do something I don't have the time for this."

She said, "I understand. What does it mean?"

"Mama Lynette please watch over me, Psalms 121. Lynette's my grandmother."

She said, "Hmm, interesting. Isn't that a Psalm of going out and coming in? "

"Yes, it is." I thought, oh, you know, the Bible.

She said, "Oh, so, do you?"

I laughed and said, "Of course."

She said to me, "You should take it a little bit more seriously. Don't you think Lynette is tired? "

"What did you just say?" I questioned her with a shocked look on my face.

Then she went on to say, "What does that say?"

"No, miss what did YOU just say?"

She's like, "People get tired of hearing the gospel when they're not a part of it." I just looked at her weird because that's not what she just said. But okay, now she was focused on my list of tattoos. She didn't touch them, but she pointed. And continued, "What is that for?"

Then I said, "We're going to go through all 30 tattoos that I have?"

She replied, "Why not?"

I said, "Well, my wrist says God's gift."

She said, "Yeah, you are. I can tell that you're very much gifted. You just, you're just putting up a fight. Aren't you tired?"

I said, "Sometimes."

And then she said, "What's that?" On my foot, I had on sandals. I had a musical note. I explained to her that I would survive on the piano. She said, "I think your tattoos are going somewhere today." And we both laughed,

"Yeah, all my tattoos have meaning. Even though it's not godly."

"You're like a billboard of information in front of me. Above that, it says God bless, doesn't it?"

And I said," Yeah."

"You know," she said, "you should spend time thinking about the reasons why you put them on."

"I know why I put them on. They mean something to me as I told you before."

She said, "It means something to you, trust me when you have a higher calling. Sometimes, it doesn't matter what you're doing or what you're about to do. As long as you get a teaching from it."

I asked, "You're a teacher?"

She answered, "Actually no. I'm just a preacher here for a crusade."

"Where's your crusade?" And she gave me the address and the time."

She said, "If you'd like, you can come, but I have a message for you."

I said," More than the message that you gave me already?"

"Yes. Take the time for someone to love you the way you love others. You are tired. You don't see it yet, but I see it. You are tired. Spend time on what you wrote on yourself. Spend time and study Psalm 41. I know what it says."

She recited it out loud without the Bible. "What part of that made you put that on your neck?"

The part in Psalms 41 that she referred to stated,

"All my enemies whisper together against me;

they imagine the worst for me, saying,

"A vile disease has afflicted him;

he will never get up from the place where he lies.

Even my close friend,

someone I trusted,

one who shared my bread has turned against me.

But may you have mercy on me, Lord;

raise me up, that I may repay them.

I know that you are pleased with me

for my enemy does not triumph over me.

Because of my integrity you uphold me

and set me in your presence forever.

Praise be to the Lord, the God of Israel,

from everlasting to everlasting.

Amen and Amen."

Psalm 41:7-13

She said to me, "If that's not powerful enough, look at the sinful acts you were going to complete today." She pointed toward the store I was going to. There were police and security taking two girls out of the store. I literally turned around and she was already walking away from me and I went right back out the door. The fact that she picked that up. I knew it was time for a change.

I didn't feel anything that whole day. I went home, took a shower, and I just had a relaxing day. That relaxing day turned into a relaxing week. In that relaxing week, I got a phone call from Frank and I answered. It's his thing, he always asks - "How are the kids or how are the boys?" I said that they were good. He said "I'm not calling you with good news today."

"What happened to you?"

"Oh, I'm fine." Then he said, "I'm calling to let you know that Harp passed away."

"What?!"

"Yeah, she just went to sleep and never woke up."

"When was this?"

He explained that it was early that morning. "Her husband called me probably like three or four hours ago and told me. I really want to go to her funeral."

"Okay, what's stopping you?"

"That means I would have to come back."

I said, "Okay.

"You're not going to ask me where I'm coming back from?"

I said, "Absolutely not. "

He said, "You know, if I miss her funeral, I wouldn't - I couldn't forgive myself. Is it worth my freedom?" I could hear his tone of voice falling.

I said to him, "It's a choice that you're going to have to make, a choice I can't make for you." He said, "What would you do?" I had no answer. He took a deep breath and before he said anything, I let him know I would attend in his absence.

A week later, I attended Harp's funeral – even though I swore I wouldn't go to another funeral. It was amazing, it looked like a wedding to be honest! People went up and they had amazing things to say about her and I learned a lot about Harp. The lady from the art gallery was there and she said hello to me before she went up there. She said, "The last conversation I had with Harp it was like she knew she was going to pass. She thanked us for everything and told our boss to give us a raise . She told us what to change around in the store. She had a conversation with me over tea. She told me, everybody she recommended to come to the store was special.

I had applied to work at this gallery twice. While I was doing my second interview for a summer job, Harp just looked at me and said, 'Hire her' to the store manager. I'd been working there for 6 years and even became a manager. I'll never forget Harp, and her inspirational quotes and conversations with me and the staff ." When she said 'everybody she recommended was special' it touched me in a way.

After 8 to 9 people went up to share their experiences, it was revealed that Harp owned these places. This was like a two-hour service with people from all walks of life and every culture. Italian, Chinese, Indian, white, black, big, small - when Harp's husband stood up to give a eulogy, it dawned on me that Harp didn't have any children. About 5 minutes into him struggling to get his words out, he revealed that they did have a daughter but she had passed. The big screen came on. They put up a few photos of the daughter and she was beautiful. She looked like Harp, just taller.

One of the photos was the same picture from the art gallery I first visited when the lady asked me, "What do you see?" At the time I had picked out a wrist watch and I had thought "That was the original picture of her at camp." Then they revealed a painting of Harp and her daughter. It was breathtaking. The staff went up to console Harp's husband. Everybody started to get up when the casket was coming down the aisle. I got up and walked outside the church before it passed me. There was a horse and carriage waiting to carry her along with police escorting.

When we got to the grave site, I kind of stayed back, I didn't really know anybody. But, people were friendly. Everyone was handed a small box; it had a butterfly inside. A man with a British accent shared a speech and directed that we open the box at the same time to release the butterfly before putting down the casket.

Because there were so many people there, I couldn't see when that was happening, but I heard the dirt hit the casket and it sent me into a place. I don't remember how long I blacked out for. But when I came to, there were two people, or three people, one in front of me, one on my left and one to my right. They were rubbing my back asking, "Are you okay? You were screaming and crying for help."

"I'm like, I don't need help. I'm standing right here."

"I just want to know that you're okay. " I could feel that I had been crying.

"Yeah, I'm okay."

I kind of stepped back to brush them off because I didn't want to cause more of a scene. In my head. I was saying, again? I didn't remember anything. But everything was blurry. I didn't know how long I blacked out for. There was a gentleman behind me. He spoke in French to the older lady. I didn't understand what he was saying. He tried to give me his handkerchief. The lady was still trying to console me, even though I was trying to back off. They were still trying to hold onto my arm. I assured them I was fine while talking to the lady. I received their kindness with a smile and many thanks and took the handkerchief to wipe my face. While doing so, the man said, "Dab, don't wipe, you will ruin your makeup."

It was Frank.

www.ingramcontent.com/pod-product-compliance
Lightning Source LLC
Chambersburg PA
CBHW051857160426
43209CB00039B/1978/J